MURDER & MAYHEM
JEFFERSON CITY

MURDER & MAYHEM JEFFERSON CITY

MICHELLE BROOKS

THE
History
PRESS

Published by The History Press
Charleston, SC
www.historypress.com

Front cover, top left: *Kansas City Times*, June 23, 1898; *top center*: Bob Kraus; *top right*: Missouri State Archives; *bottom*: Sue Ferber.
Back cover: Cole County Historical Society.

First published 2023

Manufactured in the United States

ISBN 9781467152273

Library of Congress Control Number: 2023932159

Thank you to my husband, Stephen Brooks. He has supported me in this new chapter of my life, providing monographs of Jefferson City history. In fact, he helped spark my interest in local history while I was a younger reporter. And he has been an enthusiastic assistant in preparing Murder & Mayhem Jefferson City. *It was his interest in true crime and Missouri State Penitentiary history that incited this project.*

CONTENTS

FOREWORD

I n today's world, we race to accomplish the tasks we feel must be done in our daily lives. We have little time to read, study or take notice of the history of our community and the lives of the men and women who made history.

Daily newspapers are relics of the past, due to the instantaneous connections we have through our electronic devices.

Every community, like its citizens, has a history. History connects us to our past, our future and to one another. We should embrace it. The City of Jefferson is no exception. For almost two hundred years, history has been made each day in the small Capital City of Missouri. There have been events of triumph and tragedy.

Author Michelle Brooks, a well-known former newspaper reporter and feature writer, is well-versed in the events and elements that made daily Capital City news. Through her ever-expanding interest in history, Brooks creatively brings to the student of local history the people and events that, for whatever reason, became murder and mayhem in the Capital City.

With her skills as a journalist and historian, Brooks shares the stories that made Capital City headlines in the nineteenth and early twentieth centuries. From events of the Civil War to escapes from behind the walls of the oldest prison west of the Mississippi River, she connects the reader with names we see etched in local cemeteries.

There are families living in the city today who were impacted by the events brought to life by Michelle Brooks.

She makes us aware that we are each a part of history and that our story, through triumph or tragedy, may some day be linked to murder and mayhem.

Slow down, sit down, relax, turn the lights down low and enjoy *Murder & Mayhem Jefferson City* by Michelle Brooks.

—Mark S. Schreiber

PREFACE

Those who remember my writing from the *Jefferson City News Tribune* will recall that I was a feature writer and general assignment reporter covering topics like schools, historic preservation and faith communities. Rarely did an editor assign me to a story involving murder or mayhem.

The stories in this book may not be inspiring or cheerful, but they certainly impacted the community. And these events had life-changing consequence for many people and families. Though from a darker part of our shared past, these stories are part of history nonetheless.

With true crime being a popular subject in recent decades, it seemed fitting to record some of that part of Jefferson City's past.

ACKNOWLEDGEMENTS

T hank you for the invaluable review, insight and research provided by Kyrstin Keim, Walter Schroeder, Mark Schreiber, Randy Turner, Lena Evers-Hillstrom, John Dougan, Nancy Thompson, Jenny Smith, Wayne Johnson, Deborah Goldammer, Mark Schleer and Ithaca Bryant, Jeff Patrick, Pete Oetting, Charles Machon, Springfield-Greene County Library, Pete Oetting, Patti Schmutzler, Patsy Galbreath, employees of the State Historical Society of Missouri, the Cole County Historical Society library, Central Church archives, and the volunteers at the Missouri State Archives.

I would also like to note the benefits of previous work by Sean Rost, Gary Kremer, Mark Schreiber, Walter Schroeder, Jerry Jeffries and untold newspapermen.

Thank you to those who provided photos, including Kevin Kolkmeyer, Bob Kraus, Sally Powell, Missouri State Archives, Cole County Historical Society, Lincoln University Archive, Jefferson City Police Department and Sue Ferber.

PART I

MURDERS

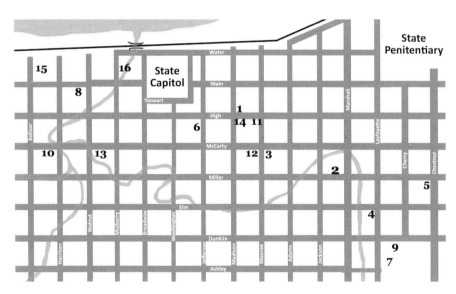

The following are estimated locations covered in Part I.

1. Burr home
2. Burr hanging
3. Old Cole County Jail
4. Bill's Café
5. Turner home
6. Rankin Taxi Service
7. Lincoln Park
8. Tritsch Restaurant
9. Lincoln University

10. Charley Brown home
11. Dr. Amos office / Parisian Hat Shop
12. Standard Oil station
13. Brennan shooting
14. Berri Drug Store
15. Kolkmeyer quarry
16. Wilcox execution

Map credit: Stephen Brooks.

1
SALLY BURR

DEATH BY CRUSHED GLASS

The first murder in Jefferson City not involving the notorious Missouri State Prison was one of shock that almost went unnoticed.

Young Sally Burr had been ill during the winter of 1841–42. She and her husband, Dedimus Buell Burr, lived in a small frame house on the north side of the 200 block of East High Street, where they were known to argue frequently. While administering Sally's medicine, Dedimus had secretly been adding crushed glass to her food.

Sally, twenty-nine, died on February 14, 1842. During the funeral procession, Dedimus Burr's apprentice asked someone if crushed glass was a common ingredient for mixing paint, because he had seen his boss crushing it in the back of the carpentry shop. The question sparked suspicions that led to an autopsy, which found "a considerable quantity of pounded glass in her stomach and bowels, sufficient to cause death," the *Boone's Lick Times* reported.

Dedimus Burr was the youngest son of a War of 1812 veteran and was left orphaned at age three. His brother-in-law, John Clark, became his second guardian after his maternal grandfather, Dedimus Johnson, died when he was twenty.

John Clark was a master stonecutter, which may be where Burr learned his carpentry skills. The Clarks, who had been Congregationalists, were baptized into the Church of Jesus Christ of Latter-day Saints after Mormon missionaries arrived in 1836 in Haddam, Connecticut. The Clarks sold their land and moved the family to Kirtland, Ohio. Not long after that, they moved again, to Caldwell County, Missouri.

It is likely that this is when Burr split from the Clarks, arriving in Callaway County about 1836. Here, he married the daughter of one of the earliest American families to settle at the French trading village of Cote Sans Dessein. Mary (Williams) Burr died at age sixteen the following year and was buried with their newborn son, Samuel Collit.

Burr married South Carolina–born Sarah "Sally" Langley in March 1839 in Callaway County. The couple soon moved to Jefferson City, where Burr found plenty of work as a carpenter, woodcarver, cabinetmaker and, for a time, prison blacksmith. In 1840, the Burr household included three boarders and four enslaved people.

Burr seemed to accumulate debt, reflected in how often his name shows up in circuit court records in the eighteen months leading up to Sally's murder.

"The city has been under considerable excitement the last few days in consequence of the death of Mrs. Burr," the *Boone's Lick Times* said.

After his arrest, Burr eventually confessed his deed to his friend, local printer Albert G. Baber. Then, he sat three months in the new county jail he had helped build two years earlier at the southeast corner of McCarty and Monroe Streets with his partners James Crump and John Rogers.

A weeklong trial in May 1842 before Judge James Morrow sealed his fate. "Every opportunity was afforded for a fair and full examination into all the facts and evidence in the case. There was no hurry, no unusual excitement and no improper restraint placed over the conduct of the case," the *Jefferson Enquirer* reported.

Morrow sentenced Burr to hang on July 8, 1842. "No doubt exists in the mind of the community as to the justness of the conviction," the *Enquirer* continued. Judge Morrow's pronouncement read as follows:

> *You have been pronounced guilty of a crime, the moral enormity of which can scarcely be paralleled in the annals of fiendishness and cruelty…one of the most extraordinary features in this case is, the apparent absence of all motive for the commission of the deed—that you had a motive, and that motive the strongest that could move the foul passions of your nature, there can be no doubt. What that motive was is known, perhaps, only to yourself and your God. That a man should murder a woman, and that woman his wife whom he had sworn at the altar to love, cherish and protect, and commit that murder by the cruelest means by torture by the administration of pounded glass without a motive the most foul and revolting, no man can for a moment doubt.*

The old Cole County Jail was new when carpenter Dedimus Burr awaited his execution here. *Library of Congress*.

Governor Thomas Reynolds received but refused several requests to commute the sentence.

The gallows were built west of the Old City Cemetery, possibly where Simonsen School is today. Farmers from the outlying area circled their wagons around the area, and prison inmates were allowed to attend.

Burr was driven from the jail to the gallows in a farm wagon along the St. Louis stagecoach road named Van Buren but today known as McCarty Street.

One record indicates that Burr made no statement and died "stoically and without evident fear." Another reports that he "made a short speech… confessed, repented and expressed hope of forgiveness. [He] admonished the audience to learn from his example."

Nearly a century later, the event was still part of the community's conversation. Dedimus Burr was buried in an unmarked grave next to Sally at Woodland–Old City Cemetery.

AUGUSTUS BUSEKRUS

A FATHER GONE

A father felt his home violated and his position as a German immigrant insulted. A teenager took offense at the suggestion he had broken the law and felt entitled because of his status as a deputy sheriff.

These next-door neighbors on Atchison Street in 1876 brought verbal accusations to gunpoint. The brief feud resulted in the death of a father trying to keep his family together, despite an earlier tragedy, and an acquittal for the person who took the shot fired into his back.

The setting for this drama began in 1866, when interim sheriff Peter Meyer bought five acres of Outlot 6, just on the southern side of the city limits between Madison and Jefferson Streets. Meyer, the son of Baden immigrants to Ohio, sold one acre on the north side the following month to Andrew "August" Busekrus, a recent immigrant from Nordrhein-Westfalen.

The Civil War had just ended, and land meant opportunity. Both families were young with several children, though the Meyers were Catholic and the Busekruses Protestant.

Meyer came to Jefferson City after chasing the California Gold Rush. He had defended the city with the Forty-Second Missouri Militia during Confederate general Sterling Price's 1864 raid and then was a captain under Colonel Herman L. Bruns, who also was sheriff at the time, with the Twenty-Fifth Missouri Volunteer Infantry. Meyer completed Bruns's term as sheriff in 1866 but was defeated for election by George H. Dulle. Meyer's candidacy was harmed by suggestions in the German-language newspaper *Fortschrift* that he was a rebel and a member of a band of bushwhackers.

Sheriff Peter Meyer sold an acre of his out-lot on Atchison Street to German-speaking immigrant August Busekrus. *1869 Bird's Eye View.*

Busekrus, fifty, like many German immigrants, was a skilled craftsman. But his family had been struck by tragedy from which they never recovered. Perhaps that is why he sought land on the outskirts of town—for a carpentry shop and for peace.

In Ohio, his wife, Mary (Troesch), had been "well connected...very beautiful and highly respected. But a great calamity came upon her," the *State Journal* reported. About 1865, Mrs. Busekrus was raped, and the family chose to raise the child from that attack as their own daughter, Minnie.

Mary Busekrus was never the same, and August was protective. The rape caused Mary to go insane. "Pale and frail," she began to wander away from home into the country and identified herself with a different name, according to the *Missouri Volksfreund*. Later newspaper accounts emphasized that Minnie, who was "mulatto," was "her" child.

August Busekrus struggled to pay his debts as he fought to keep his family together. He used his property several times as collateral for loans. Just four months before his murder, Busekrus had defaulted on a promissory note for $337 and conveyed the property to Peter Meyer as trustee. He was given one year to repay the debt to his brother-in-law John C. Feil.

This is the state of mind an overworked, emotionally depleted A.A. Busekrus was in about midnight one October night in 1876, when he walked into his own bedroom to see his daughter Marie and the teenaged neighbor, James Meyer, fleeing out the window, leaving his pants behind.

With a desperate sense of protection for his fragile family and enraged by the discovery, Busekrus wrote a letter to the sheriff and his wife, suggesting that the boy had "broken into" his house and that eighty dollars was missing from his dresser.

Marie Busekrus, seventeen, was the oldest of the four Busekrus children. James Meyer, eighteen, who had been named a deputy sheriff, maintained that she had invited him in. The *Missouri Volksfreund* was quick to point out that Meyer's intentions toward young Marie were not honorable. Rather, he was noted on several occasions bragging about his conquest to his peers.

The letter, dated October 16, 1876, and written in German, was delivered by August Busekrus's ten-year-old son, Andrew.

> *I am compelled to write you a few words, since you consider it unworthy to speak with me, a poor, unfortunate man. So, I feel obliged to write you, and ask you some questions, with the hope that you would answer the questions. First, I would like to know by what right your son, James, broke into my house at midnight and what he sought in my bedroom.*
>
> *Secondly, what right do Sam and Bill have to spitefully malign my daughter Marie and to speak badly of her? When I asked the two on Friday morning whether they knew where Marie was, they just laughed derisively and said that presumably I could find Marie with the Negroes, Schrocks and Redmann, and that would be the place where she has also been before.*
>
> *A stab in the heart would not have hurt me more than that answer. Did your son perhaps think he could do what he wished with a poor girl and a poor father? Could pull me and my daughter through the filth and march right over me? Drive me completely into the ground?*
>
> *Am I in your way? Have I ever offended you? Have my children ever offended you? I know such things have never happened, and if you think you could walk over me, then I will show you that you cannot do it, and that the law protects a poor man as well as a rich man. I will start showing it today.*
>
> *And I also hope to find out who stole the eighty dollars from my bedroom.*
>
> *Your neighbor A. Busekrus*

The Busekrus home, a single-story frame house, was a "pleasant little cottage" surrounded by trees visible from the uptown area. The Meyer home was just south. Between these two residences was a fence, which prevented neither indiscretions nor murder.

By this point, Busekrus was ready for a confrontation. Likewise, the letter provoked James Meyer, but not for the question of his morality or judgmental overtones. Rather, the young deputy was set off by the accusation of breaking the law.

With both parties feeling offended and ready for a fight, James Meyer brazenly approached the gate between the properties early the next morning with his pistol at his side. Young Andrew Busekrus saw the teenaged deputy coming and told his father. While Marie watched from the kitchen, James

Meyer demanded an "explanation" from her father, who had armed himself with a hefty stick.

Young Meyer asked why Busekrus "was blowing his horn around here" and then threatened to "blow his head off if he did not quit." After a heated exchange, Busekrus threw down his nonlethal weapon and ran into the house to get his gun, which prompted Marie to shout, "For God's sake Meyer, get away from here."

As James Meyer ran back to his own home, August Busekrus emerged from his sleeping room with a rifle that was kept behind the door. Busekrus aimed and fired, but the gun was not loaded. Expecting the matter to continue, Busekrus sent his son Andrew to get more caps for his weapon.

Deputy Meyer, on the other hand, went to the Monroe House saloon, called the Mausehund. A couple hours later, he returned to the corner of Madison and Dunklin Streets, where he met up with Richard Standish, asking to borrow his double-barreled shotgun to go hunting. The pair went down to J.C. Linhardt's store, where Meyer bought ten cents' worth of no. 4 duck shot.

Neighbor John Sachs saw Meyer walk out of the store and asked about the shotgun. When Meyer said he was going hunting, Sachs asked to come along. They went into Joe Haas's saloon, at the corner of Dunklin and Jefferson Streets, for a whiskey while Meyer loaded the shotgun. Sachs observed Meyer putting too much shot into the gun and warned him that he "might shoot someone that way."

As Meyer and Sachs walked up Madison Street toward their respective homes, Meyer said, "Watch, if Busekrus comes out and says anything to me, I will give him a load." Instead, Mary Ann Meyer saw her son and called for him to come home, then took him back to the gate of the Busekrus place to try to resolve the tenuous situation. But the teenager was still carrying the overloaded, borrowed shotgun.

Busekrus had been in the eating room with Minnie, eight. Julia, ten, was in the kitchen with her older sister Marie. The "demented" mother was in the front parlor. Young Meyer resumed his questioning and threatening of August, who wouldn't back down and had questions and threats to return.

Poor Marie watched from the window. Meyer asked her to come out, but her father told her to "shut the door and stay in there." Later, her father asked her to bring out his gun, which she didn't do. At that point, Busekrus headed into the house himself with the phrase, "I will shoot you!" While turned in his doorway, Busekrus was shot in the back by James, who was still standing on his side of the gate. Busekrus fell back into his home and crawled down the hallway to the front door, where he was found facedown and without a weapon.

When Sachs heard the shot, he ran from the street to help Mary Ann Meyer take the shotgun away from the young deputy. Sachs told James Meyer to run for it, then gave the weapon to the younger Meyer son, Sam, who followed from their house.

Neighbor John Schmidt arrived soon after hearing the shot. After Julia Busekrus told him, "Jim Meyer shot my father," Schmidt notified Coroner George B. Winston. His son Dr. Willis B. Winston found forty-three duck shot wounds along the back, neck and loin of the left side of August's body.

While the two neighboring families were left in shock and had to go through the coroner's inquest, James Meyer returned to the Mausehund, where Marshal Cohagan arrested him after the inquest found him guilty of murder. Meyer seemed more upset at losing his weapon than about his guilt. He was delivered to jailer and friend Henry Eveler, and newspapermen James Regan and Martin Regan quickly signed his bond, despite citizens feeling indignant that he was free to walk about town.

The body of August Busekrus was held at the Lutheran schoolhouse on Washington Street until Reverend Christian Ludwig Haas conducted the funeral at the German Evangelical Church. "The impression of the shocking sight on the doorstep of the home remains unforgettable," Haas wrote in his journal. The "demented" mother was hardly touched by the episode, but the children were found weeping bitterly. "How difficult it was for me to conduct the funeral service at the grave of the deceased man," Haas wrote.

The underlying current of this affair had been the social divide. The Meyers were "part of the power in-group and of definite political bent," giving young James the idea that "he is superior to the hardscrabble German immigrant," local South Side historian Walter Schroeder said. "Yet, Busekrus shows he strongly believes in the American promise of 'free and equal,' regardless of one's social-economic-political standings."

Busekrus's brother-in-law John Feil paid for the funeral and for a good lawyer to help the prosecuting attorney, Joseph R. Edwards, who was also the sitting Cole County representative in the Missouri General Assembly.

The defense team comprised seven of the most notable local attorneys, likely because Sheriff Peter Meyer was "regarded with high esteem as a neighbor," the newspaper said. "Friends and influential lawyers of Meyer succeeded in having the insolent son and murderer set free by reason of claiming self-defense," Haas recalled.

Two months after the murder, it took Winston four days and 130 men to find 40 men suitable to sit as unbiased jurors, because the case was so popular. The *State Journal* called it the "most important criminal trial in the annals of this county."

At the preliminary hearing, the *State Journal* said of James Meyer: "In passing through the ordeal, he on the whole conducted himself as cooly as could be expected. Young and boyish looking, his face flushing and paling by turns, it seemed incredible that he was there as a murderer and we hardly think he realized the enormity of the crime charged against him."

Marie Busekrus's narrative was clear, straightforward and unimpeachable, though told in a sad, reproachful way, the newspaper reported. Her "eyes were cast down by the burden of speechless grief."

The initial coroner's inquest panel, which found James Meyer guilty, was composed mostly of German-speaking neighbors. Whereas two circuit court juries reflected the wealthier and influential men of the town. A December 1876 decision agreed with the inquest that the teenage deputy was guilty of first-degree murder. But the second jury, in December 1877, ended in acquittal. "A cry of indignation swept through the entire town," Reverend Haas wrote.

The *State Journal* concluded: "A man's home is his castle, though it may be humble, though the winds may blow through it and its roof may shake in the story. Yet, a man may come near it except by his consent. It is his castle and he has a right to defense [of] it. If the defendant wanted to appease the old man's anger toward him and settle peaceably the aggrievance old man, why did he go there armed?"

While the courts pursued justice for the Busekrus family, its young members passed through various households. Immediately following the event, the children found "friendly shelter and protection under the roof of" John and Mary Atwinger, Austrian immigrants who lived with their four children a block over from the Busekrus home.

The Busekrus children then stayed with the widow of Reverend Anton Rieger, who had helped raise Busekrus's sister. Eventually, Julia entered a St. Louis orphanage, "certainly with better care and training than with an irresponsible and incapable mother." Andrew was apprenticed to a watchmaker, and Minnie became a house servant.

The outcome fell heaviest on young Marie, who went to live with family in Warren County. Immediately after the crime, she was a "raving maniac, haunted with a bloody spectre," pulling out her hair and tearing her clothes in frantic fits. "To those who knew her as a once-beautiful girl, her present condition as the merest wreck of her former self was indeed pitiable," the newspaper said.

Haas put some blame on Marie, "who was not innocent of the crime because of her carelessness and had thereby brought unutterable tragedy to an entire family."

As for the wife and mother, Mary Busekrus, the county court elected to send her to the state asylum, at its own expense, just a few weeks after the murder. But the order was rescinded, and she was taken to the county poor farm. By August 1877, she was no longer at the farm but living again at the family home, with the county court providing her with "necessities of life." The *State Journal* reported that she was "sadly demented" and in a "deplorable condition" while she continued to care for the two youngest children.

"What a person in her condition of mind will do, either of harm to the children or the premises she inhabits, cannot be told. That she is liable to do some act of violence at any time, all who know her believe," the newspaper speculated. She was returned to the county poor farm, from which she wandered off on several occasions.

James Meyer remained in Jefferson City for the rest of his life. Eight months after his acquittal, he married Alwina Staihr, who had testified at his trial. They lived with her mother at 620 Jefferson Street, and he worked as a bookkeeper and later a prison guard, alongside his father, who was not reelected sheriff as a "truly just retribution," according to Haas.

The same month as James Meyer's acquittal, the late carpenter's one-acre property was sold on the courthouse steps to his brother-in-law John Feil. The site became part of the E.H. Hutchinson subdivision, adjacent to what became the Louis C. Lohman estate, now the Salvation Army.

3

OFFICER WALLACE LAWSON

FIRST JEFFERSON CITY POLICEMAN KILLED ON DUTY

A t the bottom of the Lincoln University hilltop campus lies the African American commercial district, or "The Foot." It sprang up in the early twentieth century to serve the neighborhood around it as well as those coming from out of town to attend the "Black Harvard of the Midwest."

By 1933, the Jefferson City Council had decided that a Black police officer would better serve the African American neighborhood. This was a time before law enforcement training and experience were prerequisites to serve. Instead, most police officers were selected according to political party and popularity.

Wallace Lawson was a popular barbecue man when he was named the Black police officer to the Lafayette Street beat. When an assailant fired both barrels of a twelve-gauge shotgun at close range on April 4, 1934, Lawson became the first Jefferson City police officer killed in the line of duty.

Lawson was born in Cole County in 1877 to parents who had moved from Callaway County to the Taos area. When Lawson was fourteen, his father, James, was murdered. His body was discovered about three hundred yards from his team and wagon, near a tie camp called Padgett Hollow in Miller County, with a gunshot wound in his right side. "He was regarded as a good man here at his home," the *Cole County Democrat* reported. A white man named Thompson was attributed with the murder and caught in January 1891. James Lawson had been handling ties for a contractor named Nelson, but there was "a bitter enmity among the white tie haulers and choppers against him."

Officer Wallace Lawson was the first Jefferson City policeman to die in the line of duty, while pursuing a suspect in 1934. *Jefferson City Police Department.*

By 1900, the family had moved to 1101 Elm Street, where Wallace Lawson supported his mother and four siblings as a day laborer. He married Sadie Belle (Ellis) in 1906 and worked odd jobs to support them and their three children living on Locust Street.

"Lawson was one of the best-known barbecue cooks in Central Missouri and was in demand for big affairs. He had few equals in barbecuing meats and probably officiated at more affairs of that kind than any man of his race in this section," the newspaper said.

In January 1934, Lawson was in charge of a "big rabbit barbecue" at the Oberman building on High Street hosted by the police department as a goodwill gesture. In addition to five hundred rabbits shot by policemen and their friends, one hundred gallons of beer were provided. A dance was held free to the public.

Lawson was first appointed as an officer to the Lafayette Street District in the spring of 1933 and was reappointed in April 1934. Chief John Bruner said that Lawson was "a good policeman. He was calm when a steady hand was needed and handled his difficult beat with credit to the department. He had the respect of the people of his own race and made the ideal policeman."

Calls of rowdy behavior on late nights along Lafayette Street's cafés and nightclubs were not uncommon. About 1:00 a.m. on April 2, 1934, James Turner was with a woman at Bill's Café on Lafayette Street when he "became boisterous and attacked Monroe Bledsoe, a waiter. The two were wrestling when Mrs. Vinetia entered the place and put a stop to it," a newspaper reported.

Lawson heard the commotion from outside the café, entered and told Turner to keep quiet. Witnesses said Turner began to argue with Lawson, who slapped Turner in the face and told him to "go home or he would jail him." Turner left the café, walked across the street and then cursed Lawson. As the policeman moved toward Turner again, Turner ran east on Miller Street to his home on the southwest corner with Chestnut.

In his testimony, Turner said that Lawson used a short club called a blackjack on him and was saying, "I am tired of your bullying around here." Witnesses supported Turner's claim that Lawson was carrying a blackjack as he left the restaurant.

Clayton Thomas, Malcolm Griffin, Clementine Cove and Maybelle Brooks were standing on the porch of 830 East Miller Street when Turner came running up the porch saying that he was being pursued by a policeman. "He said it was either him or the policeman and they were going to have it out," they told the newspaper.

Thomas and Griffin tried to dissuade Turner from grabbing his loaded shotgun. But Turner searched for more shells until someone yelled, "Here he comes now," and everyone entered the house.

The small frame home sat about four feet below street level. Lawson stepped onto the porch as Turner ran around from the back of the house, where the yard was even lower than the porch. Turner's testimony said that Lawson stepped onto the porch, saying, "I am going to kill you." To which Turner replied, "Oh, no you're not."

Accounts differed at this point. Turner said Lawson fired first. The official account stated that Turner fired the first shot at Lawson without warning, most of it glancing off Lawson's Sam Brown belt buckle.

The police assessment noted that this is when Lawson drew his revolver and advanced on Turner, who fired again, striking Lawson in the heart. Lawson's gun was missing two shells. One account said he fired into the ground when he was wounded; the other noted that he fired at Turner.

The officer struggled up the slight incline, collapsing on Miller Street, where he died before neighbors could reach him. Lawson was fifty-six, leaving behind his mother, wife and five children.

As for Turner, he left the shotgun inside the house before running west to the Central Hotel, where he was a bellboy. He asked for his five dollars in pay and told the night clerk he had just killed a policeman. The clerk thought he was joking, until police questioned him the next day.

About a month earlier, Turner had been wounded by gunshot on the side of his head at the hotel. Although he said it was accidentally self-inflicted, the details were sketchy. The bullet struck him in back of the ear, creased the side of his head and glanced off. The police could not find the gun or bullet.

Back at Bill's Café, police placed twenty people under arrest and questioned them until late in the morning. Prosecuting Attorney Elliott Dampf took sworn statements, and Coroner R.E. Weaver arrived from Russellville to examine Lawson's body.

Chief John Bruner brought in every man to work overtime to find Turner. A reward of $850 was collected overnight for Turner's capture. By noon that day, more than one hundred pictures of Turner had been sent across the state.

Rumors of his whereabouts put him in a boxcar to Belle, where he held men at gunpoint. However, he sent a postcard to his wife saying he was in Kansas City but planning to turn himself in. Turner eventually arrived voluntarily at the Jefferson City police station, then in Bragg Hall, accompanied by Tony Eveler and Mike Michelson, who requested half of the reward.

While in custody in Jefferson City, James Turner was slapped by officers Horace Debo and George Vandament, after they attempted to search him. Turner "curled his lip impudently and…half rose as if to resent it." Chief Bruner defended his officers: "A face slapping is not much of a penalty for killing a policeman."

Prosecuting Attorney Dampf wanted to keep the preliminary hearing quiet, but the defense team of H.P. Lauf and State Senator William Irwin brought more witnesses than the state had summoned and demanded to see the affidavits taken after the killing. The defense's position was, "Lawson was a bully and that he had frightened and intimidated Turner to a point where the latter believed his life was in danger."

Early testimony suggested that Lawson had a reputation for being quick with a gun, including his acquittal on self-defense for killing a Mr. Davis in 1911 and another time he struck a man on the head with his gun. After his preliminary hearing, Turner was taken to the receiving cell at the Missouri State Penitentiary for safekeeping.

While the justice system was processing Turner, the community was left to fill the void of Lawson's death. Nearly six hundred people crowded into the small Church of God on Locust Street for Lawson's funeral service; many of the mourners were white, including Mayor Means Ray, Prosecuting Attorney Dampf, Chief Bruner and several fellow policemen. The Reverend Cotter delivered a tribute to Lawson's faithfulness to duty, family and friends, and the city council unanimously approved paying the funeral expenses. Of Lawson, the mayor said, "I have never known a truer man or one who was more devoted to his duty."

The city appointed Booker Mason as Lafayette Street's new Black policeman. Most city officials felt a Black officer was better suited to the Lafayette Street beat than a white officer. However, a few thought "the experiment has never been successful." In the end, Mason remained on the job through integration. "The integrity and ability of Mason has never been questioned by those known to doubt the wisdom of the appointment. They say that if a colored man is to be appointed, Mason is as good as could be found among the Democrats of that section."

At Turner's trial, a month after the incident, his attorney said Turner acted in defense of himself and his home. The prosecution noted that Lawson gave Turner every consideration: "He believed it better to correct and rebuke Turner and send him home to his wife and child than to lodge him in jail or place him in a position to be fined to pay out money which rightfully belonged to his family. He thought he could better serve the interests of law and order in that way. As reward for that consideration, Wallace Lawson was shot to death."

City Attorney June Rose pointed out that if Turner had stayed in his house instead of coming out to do battle, they would not have been in the courtroom at all. "But, he was a tough guy and he wanted a fight," Rose said.

Turner spoke in his own defense and "withstood a grilling by the state without weakening his testimony." He declared "it was either kill or get killed."

Found guilty of manslaughter, Turner was sentenced to five years at hard labor. His attorneys did not appeal. At the jail later, Turner said, "I guess maybe I'm lucky at that."

A year after Turner completed his five-year sentence, he again was charged with carrying a dangerous and deadly weapon. Turner claimed he was being threatened. But Harold Bartley had called the police, saying Turner had threatened to do him bodily harm. Police found Turner walking quickly down the street with a revolver. The following year, Turner was sentenced to six months in the county jail for assault after slashing his wife with a knife.

4

"BUD" RANKIN

A BASEBALL STAR TAKEN

The residual of a lover's quarrel took the life of a beloved taxi driver's son in 1926.

Sidney "Bud" Rankin, twenty-four, married Columbia schoolteacher Dorothy Kimbrell in August 1925. He was the son of well-liked African American taxicab owner Heber Rankin and was being groomed to take over his father's business at 306 Jefferson Street.

Heber Rankin was "one of the best known and most highly respected of the colored population here." And his son was building a similar reputation. A *Jefferson City Democrat* editorial said he "stood high in the community…a young man of exemplary habits, an asset to his race and respected by the white people, as well as the colored population."

The younger Rankin attended Lincoln University, where he had been a popular musician and star football player. In 1926, Bud Rankin was star centerfielder for the local Black baseball team, the Mohawks.

His young wife, who was completing the school year in Columbia, traveled to Jefferson City on weekends. One Sunday in May 1926, one of her former beaus also came to Jefferson City from Columbia to see Bud Rankin, but for a much different purpose.

That afternoon, the Mohawks had played a game against the Columbia team at Lincoln Park on Lafayette Street. Young Rankin had played a great game, and afterward, he and Dorothy went to his father's office to relax. It was there that John T. Scott found them at about 7:30 p.m. Scott had served in a field hospital company during World War I and "suffered from a peculiar feeling about the head" ever since. In Columbia, he had worked as a street laborer and a taxi driver and for a cleaning business.

On this Sunday, Scott had hired Columbia taxi man Gus Jackman to bring him to Jefferson City. After the game, Scott and Emmett Williams stopped at Heisinger's garage to ask where they could find Bud Rankin. Then, Scott had Jackman drive him to the Jefferson Street office and stay in the car with the engine running.

Scott walked into the front of the business, where Heber Rankin was seated. Scott asked if Bud was in, and the father said he was in the office. The killer walked in and called Bud aside, and "without a word of warning, he whipped out a pistol and began shooting."

The first bullet struck Bud in the hand. When the victim turned, Scott shot him through the side. Dorothy, who was seated just a few feet from her husband, started toward Bud. Scott, her former beau, shot her in her wrist and then the abdomen.

The elder Rankin ran in after hearing the shots and saw his son, who said, "Oh, Dad, he's killing us." While Heber lifted his son with one arm, Scott put the gun to the elder's neck. The last to be fired at, Heber Rankin managed to strike Scott's arm just as he pulled the trigger. The potentially fatal bullet passed over his shoulder. With that, Scott struck the taxi owner with the pistol and ran out to his waiting Columbia taxi for his getaway.

The entire event took less than one minute.

Traffic Officer Erhardt was first on the scene, followed by hundreds of onlookers. Erhardt sent the wounded to St. Mary's Hospital and notified the Boone County sheriff.

After dropping Scott off in Columbia, Jackman returned to Jefferson City for more passengers. But by that time, law enforcement had set up a roadblock and advised him to turn back, "because there had been a shooting scrape."

Scott was seen at a Columbia restaurant with Williams just an hour after the attack. The latter then drove Scott to Boonville, where the murderer boarded a train to Sedalia. Police arrested Williams that day, suspecting him as the getaway driver before learning that it was Jackman who drove the car to Columbia.

Bud Rankin died at 9:45 a.m. the next day. Before that, he was able to tell Prosecuting Attorney Sam Haley and Policeman Al Schatzer that he had never had trouble with Scott before. But, Rankin noted, "Scott had… attempted to continue his attentions to Mrs. Rankin and was repulsed."

Mohawks team manager "Lefty" Robinson was one of the last to be at Bud Rankin's bedside. The victim told Robinson that Scott had threatened him: "I said you would never live to be happy, if you married that girl."

While Dorothy was still in the hospital, not expected to live, Bud was among the first to be buried, in Longview Cemetery. The funeral was held at the family home, 430 East McCarty Street, by Reverend E.L. Scruggs.

Hundreds attended what the *Jefferson City Tribune* reported was the "largest [funeral] in the history of any colored man in city history." Members from the Mohawks served as pallbearers, and a memorial was held at Lincoln Park, where the team wore black crepe on their uniforms.

By the fourth day after the shooting, Dorothy's condition was slightly improved, and the county court had set a $300 reward for information to catch Scott. Jackman was charged as an accessory after the fact, though Scott validated the taximan's claim of not knowing Scott's intentions when he drove him to the Rankin taxi office.

Nevertheless, Jackman heard the shots and knew what had happened. Scott got back into the idling taxi, saying, "I just shot two *&#*, so get me back to Columbia quick." Jackman's defense was that he "feared Scott would kill him, if he did not comply with his orders." But Scott said Jackman also had a revolver and drove away from the crime scene of his own free will.

At his preliminary hearing, Jackman appeared "greatly agitated and so frightened that he shook as though afflicted with the ague.…[He] twisted his hands nervously and his legs shook so violently he had difficulty maintaining his seat," the newspaper said.

A week after the shooting, Dorothy was still "tenaciously clinging to the thread of life." A committee from the Black community—Duke Diggs, C.G. Williams, "Lefty" Robinson and Frank Abbington—began raising money for a larger reward, reaching $320. Governor Sam Baker added another $300 from the state, and Heber Rankin personally offered $100 when Scott was captured.

By May 21, eleven days after the shooting, Scott's sister, Lizzie Fuller, indicated that her brother might surrender if he was assured of a fair trial. She feared that Scott's arrest would lead to a lynching, but they were "weary of the constant flight."

After another three weeks, Scott finally was located, thanks to a call from Alta Johnson in Muskogee, Oklahoma. She had known Scott from living in Columbia and ultimately received the $1,000-plus reward.

Two days after Dorothy miraculously left the hospital for her home in Columbia, Sheriff Louis Withaup headed south to pick up Scott, with Prosecuting Attorney Haley and Deputy "Slim" McCullough.

On his return to the Cole County Jail, Withaup received a phone call threatening that a mob was coming for Scott. The sheriff prepared for a siege, but only Bill Burgett arrived, asking to "let me in there with Scott for a few minutes." Sheriff Withaup pulled his revolver on Burgett, defending his promise to Scott of protection. While Burgett continued to talk of a lynching, Heber Rankin arrived and told Burgett to forget about mobs. When deputies went to Lafayette Street to see if a mob was forming, they learned that the few African Americans who were still up after 1:00 a.m. thought "Burgett should be locked up for trying to start something."

Mohawks manager Robinson added, "All we ask is a speedy trial and justice for the killer."

While Scott awaited his trial, Jackman was found guilty of aiding Scott by keeping the car running and driving from the scene. Before Jackman began his three-year sentence at the Missouri State Penitentiary in July 1926, he frustrated one of Scott's many escape attempts at the Cole County Jail. When the deed was in progress, Jackman gave Sheriff Withaup the prearranged signal by lighting his lamp. Two saws were discovered in the jail, and one bar to a window had been removed.

Finally, in October 1926, Scott's trial began in Cooper County on a change of venue. More than one hundred Jefferson City residents traveled the distance for the trial. Heber Rankin had been bitterly disappointed at the decision to change the venue in September and had to be helped from the courtroom by his wife and daughter.

Scott had agreed to plead guilty if the prosecution recommended a life sentence, but they refused. Scott's reputation in Columbia had not been good. Four years earlier, he had shot and killed Ed Williams in a saloon brawl, and he was then involved with an underage girl.

At the trial, Dorothy Rankin fainted just before she was called to the witness stand and again as she stepped down. She tried to avoid looking at the defendant, who kept his eyes on her while she testified.

After a two-day trial, the jury was "hopelessly divided," and Scott's attorneys entered a plea of guilty with a sentence of life in prison. Most of the jurors held out for first-degree murder, but not one favored the death penalty. In the end, the defense said the state failed to prove premeditation.

Heber Rankin, his relatives and his friends were "manifestly disappointed at the termination of the trial." They considered the murder of Bud Rankin the "most wanton and brutal murder in the history of Jefferson City."

Jackman, the thirty-year-old cab driver, died the following month at the prison quarry. And Heber Rankin, the grieving father, died that December.

Scott was paroled in 1947 after serving only twenty-one years of a life sentence. He first sought parole in 1943, but Bud Rankin's sister, Alberta, who was secretary to the president at Lincoln University, registered her protest and circulated a petition in the community. Alberta died in 1946.

JOHN TRITSCH

SADDLEMAKER TURNED RESTAURANT OWNER SHOT

A well-respected saddletree maker, John G. Tritsch bought the Mill Bottom bakery and restaurant of Herman and Michael McKinney in 1919 after his son Robert returned from serving in a field artillery medical detachment in France during World War I.

Tritsch brought his trade from Cincinnati, Ohio, to the Sullivan Saddle Tree Company inside the Missouri State Penitentiary, where he worked twenty-five of his forty years in the industry. The family first lived near the prison but moved to the Mill Bottom, where they were well liked by their neighbors.

It is not surprising, then, that they enjoyed the same loyal patronage as the McKinney Brothers Café had developed at 509 West Main Street, with many regulars coming from the local mills and railroad roundhouse. John's wife, known in the neighborhood as Mother Tritsch, was in the family restaurant as much as her husband and son and was known for her pleasant manner and good humor.

Eighteen-year-old British balloonist William Gray entered the Tritsch Restaurant on November 12, 1923, with a hood over his head and a revolver in his hand. Neighborhood children that day had been playing cops and robbers, and Gray did not appear much older than them to friendly John Tritsch, who was standing at the counter.

"I think I know you; take off that mask," Tritsch said to the teenager. Instead, Gray pointed the weapon at the restaurant owner and told him to

Saddlemaker John Tritsch and his son bought the McKinney Brothers Café in the Mill Bottom after the latter returned from World War I. *Missouri State Archives, Mark Schreiber Collection.*

throw up his hands. Unfortunately, the saddlemaker believed that Gray was playing a prank, as the children had been doing in the neighborhood.

So Tritsch said, "Wait, I'll show you the gun we keep here," and reached down for his own firearm. Surprised, Gray shot Tritsch in the stomach, a wound he died from two days later. "The aged man, with a look of surprise and bewilderment, staggered and fell back into a chair," the newspaper reported.

Gray fled out the door without the money he had come for and ran west toward Harrison Street. Robert Tritsch, son of the victim, and a restaurant employee, Joe Schneider, followed Gray, shouting at him to stop. Gray turned back briefly to fire a few shots at the pursuers. After turning north to the river, Gray jumped in a boat, which had a leak and eventually sank. Several hours later, he was found in the old railroad tunnel by Constable John Bruner, father of the chief of police.

Waiting in the street during the attempted robbery was Osage City fisherman Emmett Kinnamon. It turns out that young Gray was greatly influenced by the forty-nine-year-old, who provided the layout of the restaurant; the pistol, which came from the Jefferson City Sand Company office across the street; and liquor to motivate Gray into action. When Gray fled after the shooting, Kinnamon calmly returned to his car and Osage City, where he was later arrested. He denied involvement in the robbery.

Gray pled guilty to murder at his preliminary hearing. At his sentencing, he admitted that Kinnamon and strong drink were to blame for his plight. The Tritsch family had demanded the death penalty, but Gray was given life in prison because of his remorse, his age and the fact that he had been influenced by an older man.

During his time in prison waiting for Kinnamon's trial, Gray learned what prisoners think of snitches, and he later refused to testify. Nonetheless, Kinnamon was convicted of complicity in the murder at the Cooper County Court in September 1924, a decision that was upheld by the Missouri Supreme Court. "We always felt that Kinnamon was more to the young fellow. If anyone was to have been hanged, it should have been Kinnamon," Robert Tritsch said on behalf of the family.

Twelve years after the crime, Gray was paroled by Governor Guy Park but was arrested by U.S. Immigration at the prison gate and sent back to England, despite protests from the Tritsch family and friends. After successfully preventing previous parole attempts, William Tritsch said: "We were told this man would stay in prison the rest of his life.…All our friends had hoped he would be kept where he could do no more harm."

The next year, in May 1936, Kinnamon escaped from the Missouri State Prison's "church farm" but was recaptured the same day. Eighteen years after the crime, Governor Forrest Donnell paroled Kinnamon from his life sentence.

Robert Tritsch continued to operate the family's restaurant until his death in 1950.

PROFESSOR ROMEO WEST

LINCOLN UNIVERSITY MURDER

The first known murder to occur on the Lincoln University campus took place in March 1918. At the time, Professor Romeo West, thirty-one, was secretary of the faculty of Lincoln Institute, which later became Lincoln University. He held several positions over the more than twenty years he was on campus.

Theodore Martin, superintendent of the school's boardinghouse, had been with the school for less than a year.

West had requested some dishes to be used for a social event, but Martin refused. West, who was known to have a quick temper and often quarreled, argued awhile and then left the room in the school dormitory.

According to Martin, West returned a few minutes later in a threatening posture and carrying an automatic pistol. This was not the first time West had threatened Martin, who had previously been nearly stabbed with a fish gig.

Fearing that his life was in danger, Martin grabbed the weapon and fired five times, three fatally striking West. Martin surrendered to the police thirty minutes after the killing, claiming self-defense. The weapon was not discovered until much later. He was released on a $3,000 bond supported by white and Black men of Jefferson City and Columbia.

West was born in St. Louis and arrived at Lincoln at age fourteen in 1893. He was a major athletic talent as a student and then coached the school's teams. He graduated from the teacher education program in 1901 and remained at Lincoln as President Benjamin F. Allen's personal secretary. He became a professor of bookkeeping and business courses in 1903, and in 1905, he became the first head librarian.

West had separated from Lincoln by 1910 and, in 1912, was principal of the Black school in California, Missouri, and serving as Lincoln Institute alumni president. By the summer of 1917, he had returned to Lincoln, about the same time Martin was appointed superintendent of the boarding department. Nine months later, West was dead.

In September 1918, Martin was found not guilty of murdering West. The *Kansas City Sun* said Martin's demeanor on the witness stand influenced the "jurors that he had killed West only in an effort to prevent West from killing him first."

Romeo West was an athlete and professor for nearly twenty years at Lincoln Institute before his death. *Lincoln University Archives.*

After exoneration, Martin thanked the community for its kindness during his time as manager of the boarding department and during his tribulation. He promised to "strive to live in the future that none shall ever have reason to feel their confidence in me misplaced."

MILLIE GAINES

CHRISTMAS DAY TRAGEDY

Cole County's first multiple hanging was in June 1898. Both criminals had appealed to the Missouri Supreme Court after being found guilty of first-degree murder in Cole County Circuit Court.

The trap for Tobe Lanahan and Edward McKenzie fell at 9:00 a.m. in the county jailyard, what today is the Jefferson City police station. More than one thousand applications had been submitted to Sheriff Francis J. Fromme to witness the executions, but he limited the audience to four hundred, including African Americans and women.

A twelve-by-sixteen-by-sixteen-foot plank fence enclosure was built around the scaffold, which had two trapdoors measuring two feet by seven feet with an eight-foot drop. New ropes were ordered from St. Louis, including two for Lanahan because of his size and weight.

In the days before the execution, McKenzie and Lanahan met with Father Otto Joseph Stanislaus Hoog, seventh pastor of St. Peter Catholic Church, and converted to Catholicism. Even Governor Lon Stephens visited with the men for an hour.

The night before, they were put in their cells at 9:00 p.m. McKenzie read Matthew 4 and then said he was ready to go. They were given a hearty breakfast early while the large crowd gathered outside.

Lanahan stepped nonchallantly up the thirteen steps of the scaffold, while McKenzie had to be carried, having suffered a stroke. Lanahan told Deputy Al Smith that he had not seen a hanging but "he expected shortly to feel one" and later told the sheriff "to hurry because he wanted to be wherever he was going in time for dinner."

Neither criminal said anything from the scaffold, though Lanahan was said to be laughing and saying "goodbye" along his approach. After their heads were covered with black caps, Sheriff Sone sprang the trap.

Waylaying a Farmer

McKenzie had waylaid a kind farmer on Lohman Road for $400. He would not have been suspected if he hadn't spent $32 before 10:00 a.m. the next day—three silk dresses for his wife and a barrel of pickles.

Stockman Nicholas Linhardt had returned from selling carloads of cattle in St. Louis on April 3, 1896, and was known to carry large sums of money on his person. Having been a sometime ranch hand for Linhardt, McKenzie knew his routines and caught him on his nightly return home from visiting neighbors.

Although arrested the next morning, McKenzie escaped. Of one-quarter Black ancestry, McKenzie had blue eyes and sandy-red hair, allowing him to pass as white when he fled to Indian Territory, where he was recognized by a deputy U.S. marshal based on photographs that had been sent out. McKenzie finally was tried in January 1898.

Murder of a Fourteen-Year-Old

Lanahan was a wide, strong, twenty-eight-year-old Black man working for Joseph Stampfli's furniture store, driving the wagon, sweeping the floors and doing heavy work. The Stampfli store was a two-story brick building with a basement in the rear, where the ground sloped.

At about 4:45 p.m. on Christmas Day, fourteen-year-old Millie Gaines had been sent by her mother to Brandenberger's Drug Store on an errand. Near Penninger's livery stable, Lanahan approached the girl, and they walked to the intersection of Jefferson and High Streets. The young girl then continued on her way east on High Street. Later, Gaines and Lanahan were seen together, with his arm around her, headed toward the alley behind Stampfli's off Jefferson Street.

Only Lanahan was seen coming out of the alley later. He spent the remainder of the night and early morning in the Monroe House bar. At 7:00 a.m., Lanahan woke up James Meyers, a clerk at Stampfli's who slept at the store, because he wanted the keys to open and begin cleaning.

The day before, Stampfli had left his store at about 10:00 a.m., and Meyers left about noon, returning at around 6:00 p.m. All of the store's doors had been locked except the porch on the alley, so Lanahan could come and go to do his work during the day.

Just inside the porch entrance was a flight of stairs to the basement. And that is where young Millie Gaines lost her life.

Meyers discovered her body on the cold alleyway just beyond the porch not long after Lanahan had awoken him. She was covered with a yellow clay-like dust mingled with her blood, and she had excelsior pieces in her hair. Both of these matched items in the Stampfli basement. It was obvious that the floor at the basement door had been recently swept.

Meyers moved the girl's body out of the alley and into the basement. He found Lanahan in the second floor and told him of the girl's murder and that Meyers suspected him of the deed. Lanahan asked Meyers to take his big knife so that Lanahan could say he sold it to him. Meyers refused, so Lanahan simply tossed the knife on top of a wardrobe in the furniture store.

Gaines had suffered blunt force trauma to the head. But it was the remainder of her wounds that defined the murder as "a crime which for its barbarity and cruelty stands unparalleled in the history of criminal jurisprudence," the Missouri Supreme Court opinion said. She had a deep knife wound in her stomach near her navel, and her external sex organs and the vaginal canal had been removed.

Lanahan had been arrested before for attempting to ravish another Black girl, just age nine, and for other crimes. After Lanahan's arrest in the Gaines case, Meyers retrieved the knife from the wardrobe for the prosecuting attorney.

The closest Jefferson City ever came to a lynching followed. Knots of Black men gathered on street corners, and as their numbers grew, their talk became more violent. The group moved to the jail at about 8:00 p.m.

It was Governor William Stone who addressed the crowd while deputies were being armed with rifles from the state's armory. Stone promised that justice would take its course and that the "Capital City must not be disgraced with a lynching." The *Kansas City Journal* reported that one thousand men stood in front of the Cole County jail at 8:30 p.m.

Tobe Lanahan.

Tobe Lanahan was hanged in 1898 for the rape and murder of a fourteen-year-old girl on Christmas Day. *Kansas City Times, June 23, 1898.*

Apparently, Stone's pleas were well spoken. The *Journal* said that the crowd applauded and dispersed afterward. Although the most prominent and influential among the Black community opposed lynching until Lanahan's guilt was clearly established, Chief of Police Frank Henderson committed to guarding Lanahan at all hazards. Stone and Mayor Edwin Silver also remained until Lanahan was taken by escort to the Missouri State Penitentiary.

"The negroes are very much worked up about the matter, and some of the most prominent of them have told Sheriff [Samuel H.] Stone that as soon as it was announced for certain that Lanahan is the right man they will lynch him and nothing he can do will keep them from it. The white people of the city are also strongly in favor of lynching," the *St. Louis Post-Dispatch* reported the next day.

The *Journal* said that "excitement among the Negroes has been at fever heat all day and on all corners they could be seen in small groups discussing the crime."

From his jail cell, Lanahan admitted to his fellow inmates that he had committed the crime, and he also made a confession to Sheriff Sone. But at his trial, Lanahan said he only lured the girl to the basement but did not commit the murder. He said a strange white man from the Central Hotel had offered him five dollars "to bring the girl over so he could use her." Lanahan said that when Gaines returned from the store, he met her again at Lohman's corner and took her to Stampfli's basement, where the strange white man was waiting. He said that was the last time he saw her alive.

Five months after the crime, a jury found Lanahan guilty of first-degree murder. The murderer displayed no emotion throughout the court appearance but trembled head to foot when the decision came out. Asked later about the verdict, Lanahan said he did not care and that they could do with him as they pleased.

He was sentenced to hang on June 25, 1897, but was granted a new trial in August. Apparently, Sheriff Sone had talked with members of the jury, offering tips on the case. It took the second jury only fifteen minutes to come to the same conclusion. The *Post-Dispatch* said it was one of the quickest verdicts ever reached in a Cole County murder case.

DR. OMAR AMOS

TANGLE OVER STEPS AND SHEDS

A doctor, a photographer and his wife, a milliner, found they could not
get along. What came between them were chickens, lumber and a
difference of opinion on who was in charge.

Dr. Omar Elton Amos operated his medical practice out of the second
floor of 229 East High Street, where he lived with his wife, Jenny, and their
son Earl.

Born the son of a well-to-do farmer near Russellville, Amos studied at
the Hooper Institute in Clarksburg before earning his medical degree from
the American Medical School in St. Louis. He first practiced in Lohman,
where he lost his first wife and son. He came to Jefferson City in 1909,
serving as county coroner and then was appointed medical examiner
during the First World War.

Amos was "well and favorably known." His "work given without
recompense among the poor of the city, endeared him to his legions of
friends," the *Daily Capital News* said.

Then, in 1922, photographer Thomas Jack Simcoe bought the building at
229 East High Street from local druggists Bed Tolson and Rube Armstrong.
His wife, Belle, opened the Parisian Hat Shop in the retail space on the main
level after purchasing the Fricke Millinery Company.

The Simcoes were born and reared in Fulton. They operated a laundry
business in Arkansas for more than a decade before T.J. Simcoe opened his
photography studio at 210a East High Street in 1912.

Immediately on the purchase, Simcoe set out to make improvements, first
cleaning out the lower floor. Then he hired carpenters Clarence Pace and

Walter Kirchner to tear down the garage, shed and back steps. From the moment Simcoe's improvements impacted the back side of the building, Amos was arguing and interfering.

Thomas Simcoe considered the back lot unsanitary and a fire trap because of chickens, trash and a garage, all belonging to the Amos family.

Amos tried to run off a potential renter for the building's basement. When L.M. Wilson showed up to look at the location, Amos told him that he had charge of the basement, where his things were. Wilson said he thought Simcoe owned the building, to which Amos said, "If Mr. Simcoe wanted to remain all together, he had better stay away."

The matter increased in severity one Wednesday afternoon in January, when the Simcoes from the backyard and the Amoses from their second-story porch shouted at one another. In the end, Mrs. Amos threw a board at Thomas. It missed him and made a terrible wound on Belle's hip.

Two days later, Mrs. Simcoe saw from her millinery store that Dr. Amos once again had interrupted the work of carpenters her husband had hired and called him at his studio.

Mr. Simcoe had directed the carpenters to tear down the rotting rear steps and the outbuildings at the end of the lot. Amos told the workers to build the steps wider. In the previous arguments, Amos had insisted, "I will build it out of the kind of lumber I feel like and make it as long and wide as I want." To this, Simcoe called Amos a liar and said, "You are not going to put it up that way."

On this January afternoon, Simcoe arrived in the back of the property, where "hot words followed," causing Mrs. Simcoe to call Policeman Al Walthers. Amos told Simocoe, "you go to H--- and don't you speak to me anymore," to which Simcoe replied that he would speak to him whenever he wanted to. The policeman saw the two men quarreling as he approached.

Amos jumped down from the second-story porch, knocking Simcoe into a chicken coop. Then the doctor jumped on top of the photographer. The policeman tried to separate the men, but Dr. Amos got out of the officer's grip and ran at Simcoe again.

This time, Simcoe had pulled out a revolver and fired at Amos, but the shot missed. Again, Officer Walthers had hold of Amos, and again the doctor got away. It was the last time he rushed for Simcoe, who fired a second time. After his shot landed, Simcoe did not resist turning over the gun to Walthers. Simcoe later admitted that he was carrying the .32-caliber pistol because he feared trouble with Amos.

The charges changed from assault to murder after Amos died five days later following emergency surgery. Members of the Odd Fellows and Masons, as well as the city's doctors, turned out for his funeral at Cole Springs Church.

Until his trial, Simcoe continued to operate his photography studio, including the composites for the Fifty-Second General Assembly.

A jury finally heard the case three months after the shooting, and Judge Henry Westhues discharged the jury when a verdict couldn't be reached between manslaughter and second-degree murder.

Not long after the murder suit was resolved, Belle Simcoe became ill with cancer. Capital Saddlery moved into her millinery store by May 1923. Belle died in 1924, and then Thomas Simcoe moved back to Fulton.

9

VICTOR BLOCK

ALMOST UNBELIEVED CONFESSION

A forty-four-year-old father of four, Victor Block drove to town from his Elston farm to work as filling station attendant at the Standard Oil station at the corner of Monroe and McCarty Streets. The snowy day in February 1942 seemed like any other winter's day.

That a twenty-one-year-old might hold up the station to impress a girl, much less fatally shoot him, surely didn't cross Block's mind. And yet, Warren McConville walked into the station with a .38-caliber pistol and shot Block in the chest. The snow covered McConville's footprints, and no witnesses were found. The mystery might never have been solved but for a voluntary confession a few months later. "McConville's confession to St. Louis police was so theatrical there was some doubt he was the hold-up slayer he claimed to be," the *Globe-Democrat* said.

McConville was on his way from Holden to St. Louis, where he hoped to find a job. He took a revolver from a family member and bought cartridges for it at the Holden hardware store. Empty shells were found at his home, where he had shot them in target practice.

He bought a train ticket to Jefferson City, planning to make money to get to St. Louis with a holdup. While staying at a hotel in the Capital City, he met a girl. They had several drinks, and she encouraged him to rob the store and give her half the take.

In McConville's May 1942 confession, he said: "I was groggy from liquor when I left a hotel in Jefferson City near the railroad station and walked a short distance to the filling station. The man was alone, I pulled out the gun and told him to turn over his money. He opened the cash register and told me to help myself. I took out about $18 and then I saw the man reach in back of the safe. I thought he was trying to get a gun. Then, I fired once and turned, ran, and dropped the gun in the Missouri River." (The weapon was found a month later in a railroad lake near Holden.)

The murderer remained in Jefferson City overnight. He read about his deed in the morning newspaper and then continued on to St. Louis. McConville never saw the girl from the Capital City hotel again. He might have kept his secret had it not been for another girl.

He completed his trip to St. Louis, where he found work as a shoe factory clerk. There, he met coworker Rosemary Cummings, who turned down his proposal of marriage. The rejection sent him to voluntarily confess his earlier crime to a St. Louis night watchman, and he then signed a written confession, three months after the murder.

The *Globe-Democrat* described McConville as a "dreamy-eyed, small-town youth." McConville was insistent on the death penalty, despite officers telling him that he was too young to want to die. His reply was, "Young in years, but not in mind," the *Globe-Democrat* reported.

He also was not shy about sharing his shame with the press. "I want to make a statement to all young people who have crime in mind. Crime does not pay. I, as an example, have turned myself over to the law to save my soul in view of our God. Also, never, never touch intoxicating liquor and make sure you do not lose your head over the female sex. I feel I have relieved my mind in giving this statement."

Before McConville left his hometown of Holden, he tried to enlist in the U.S. Army but was rejected because of a childhood case of infantile paralysis. He had worked odd jobs since graduating high school and had some minor encounters with the law, but nothing serious.

McConville pled guilty, and Judge Sam Blair sentenced him to life at the Missouri State Penitentiary, recommending no mercy to the sentence later. The judge called the gas chamber "the easy way out" and then chastised the youth for seeking publicity and recognition for his crime. "Maybe this man is remorseful and penitent.…To me, he looks just about as cool as a frozen fish," Blair added.

Twelve years after being sent to prison, McConville was among twenty-two convicts indicted for their roles in the historic 1954 riot. He was charged with malicious destruction of property, battering down doors, breaking windows and wrecking cell blocks. He was sentenced to an extra five years, which he never had the chance to serve.

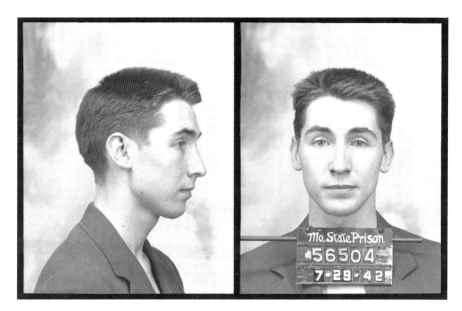

Warren McConville would have gotten away with murder if not for a girl and a guilty conscience. *Missouri State Archives, Missouri State Penitentiary mugshots.*

Four years after that, McConville was fatally stabbed. The thirty-seven-year-old had been in a fight with Gordon Lee Cooper, sentenced to life from Butler County for armed robbery. The two developed a problem after McConville stole an elderly inmate's watch. The old man was a friend of Cooper, who threatened McConville until he returned it.

McConville then vowed to "get" Cooper. He chose November 29, 1958, as they were leaving the dining hall. McConville and his friends had knives drawn. When Cooper drew out a larger knife, the three friends abandoned the attack.

In the tunnel area near the dining hall, McConville and Cooper fought with sharpened files smuggled out of a workshop. McConville did not survive his wounds. When no one claimed his body, it was sent to the American School of Osteopathy at Kirksville.

10

ROBERT BRENNAN

WHEN "HALLOO-ING" WENT TOO FAR

The Henry Kolkmeyer quarry was active in 1878, creating railroad ballast and bringing new people to town for jobs, like Robert Brennan, a twenty-four-year-old who arrived in January.

Quarry coworkers George Opel, Emil Smith and Brennan went uptown for entertainment at about 9:00 p.m. on April 30, 1878. Over two hours, they had a beer at Joe Huegel's, a beer and cigar at Schott's and two beers at Chris Hoechenroeder's, where they played three games of pigeon hole.

As the three young men returned west to their Mill Bottom homes, they were full of life and vigor. They were walking on the north side of High Street when Brennan let out a "halloo" in front of Captain Charles Maus's store at the corner of Jefferson Street and another near McCarty's old livery, now part of the Capitol grounds. As the trio continued, Officer John Cohagan, who was standing near City Hotel at the corner of Madison Street, heard their boisterous behavior and began to follow.

"I did not think he had made noise enough to attract attention," Opel later said.

When the boys reached the corner with Washington Street, across from the Thomas Lawson Price mansion, Cohagan approached, causing Opel to run north on Washington Street toward the Capitol. The officer pursued Opel, and Brennan followed them, but Smith continued down High Street.

When Cohagan caught Opel, Brennan shouted, "What are you running at that man for?" A scuffle ensued, and Brennan threw the officer in the gutter.

The Kolkmeyer quarry, which sat roughly in the block bounded by Bolivar and Harrison, Main and the river, was popular during railroad expansion. *Kevin Kolkmeyer.*

Brennan continued on his way home, passed the convent on the corner with Broadway and passed Herman Haar's home. Cohagan lost interest in Opel and took off after Brennan.

Fellow quarryman John Hartman was coming from the other direction on High Street. Hartman stopped to exchange pleasantries with Brennan about the weather and the people dancing at the wedding party at Christ Kolkmeyer's house. Then Brennan continued west on High Street toward Mulberry.

Just as Hartman had taken a few more steps east, he was passed by Cohagan, who caught Brennan by the arm and jerked him around. Hartman never heard the police officer say Brennan was under arrest or give him other orders. Others from the party said they heard Cohagan say, "If you cut at me again, I will shoot you."

A short scuffle followed, ending with the "sharp report of a pistol and the falling of Bob Brennan to the ground," the *State Journal* reported. Standing over Brennan, Cohagan asked, "What did you cut at me for?" To which Brennan answered, "I never cut at you." At that point, Cohagan was "still pointing the pistol excitedly at him and in the direction of the house." John Hartman approached him and asked that he not shoot at the house.

Then Hartman asked Cohagan why he had shot Brennan. The officer's reply was something to the effect of, "He was hallooing and yelling up town and he had had it with him."

Brennan adamantly denied having a knife until his dying breath. Partygoers led by Fred Kolkmeyer Jr. got lamps and looked around for the weapon. Bill Heinrichs, whose family owned the furniture and undertaking business, was the only one willing to search the victim's vest and pants.

Curiously, Cohagan only showed the cut marks in his clothes after leaving the scene.

Someone fetched Reverend Otto Hoog, pastor of St. Peter Catholic Church, and three doctors soon arrived: Dr. Tennessee Mathews and Dr. William A. Curry, followed closely by Coroner Dr. Willis Winston. They all examined Brennan and found that the ball had entered his abdomen, causing fatal damage.

The partygoers built a litter and carried Brennan to his attic room at Christ Kolkmeyer's boardinghouse, at the corner of Mulberry and McCarty Streets, where Father Hoog took confession and Brennan lived a week with his wounds. Brennan told Hoog, "I did not come to Jefferson to be shot down like a dog."

At 10:00 a.m. the next day, the prosecuting attorney and judge took Brennan's statement. He maintained that he never had a knife and that he had no quarrel with Cohagan. Opel concurred: "Bob never had a knife.… He generally borrowed a knife from the foreman, when he needed one."

The officer was found guilty of felony murder by a coroner's inquest. His bond was put up by four major forces in Jefferson City's community: druggist and hotelier Tennessee Mathews, hotelier and postmaster William G. McCarty, hotelier Fred Knaup and builder Fred Binder. He then resumed his law enforcement duties.

John Cohagan had been the city night watchman and then deputy marshal under his brother Charles, who was appointed city marshal by Mayor Charles McCarty in 1872. The brothers had emigrated from Prussia with their parents in 1853 and came to Jefferson City in 1863.

Cohagan was charged with first-degree murder in December 1878 and died two years later at age forty. His gravestone at Woodland–Old City Cemetery notes that he was the deputy city marshal.

11

AMALIA BERRI

SIBLING MURDER-SUICIDE

Two suicides surrounded Amalia (Hofius) Berri, who was left to operate the family drugstore by her husband and who was gunned down by her brother.

Born in Radevormwald, Rheinland, Amalia emigrated at age sixteen after the death of her father, traveling with her brother-in-law Peter Clarenbach through New Orleans to St. Louis. There, she met druggist Fredrick Berri, seventeen years Amalia's senior, when he arrived from Switzerland four years later.

By 1850, the Berris had set up one of the earliest drugstores in Jefferson City in a two-room log cabin at the southeast corner of Madison and High Streets. Their business was quite successful and continued through the Civil War, even receiving dispensation from the provost marshal for the limited sale of liquor.

Despite being a prosperous druggist, Fredrick committed suicide with a pistol in May 1865. That left Amalia to operate the popular store. While two sisters and her mother also settled in Jefferson City, it was her younger brother Edward Hofius, who had been working in California, whom she called on for help after Fred's death.

Amalia continued to grow the business, taking in her niece Mary Clarenbach as a housekeeper and boarder.

One night in 1872, neighbors heard the discharge of firearms in the apartment above the corner drugstore. When they arrived, Amalia was on the floor, mortally wounded, and Edward was upstairs with a bullet through his brain.

Edward had attended a picnic where a lady may have rejected his attentions. When he returned home, Amalia invited him to share supper. Edward turned down the offer and instead complained that since his return from California, "she had not done for him what she ought to have done pecuniarily," according to the niece. He demanded money that Amalia was holding for him and said he was leaving.

As Edward went to his upstairs room, Amalia followed him, still in conversation. He turned and pulled out a pistol. She turned and was shot in the back two inches above the hip. Amalia survived the painful wound long enough to make her will.

Young Mary Clarenbach found her aunt on the floor after hearing the pistol fire. She rushed forward to take the pistol from her uncle, who fired at her twice, missing. Then he put the weapon to his own head and fired. The first shot passed through his hat. The second shot went through his left eye socket. "The brain oozed out; he continued insensible for a short time, and then died," the *People's Tribune* reported.

The newspaper continued: "It is evidence that there is some cause back of this which is not yet revealed, although a thousand surmises are given.… Both he and his sister had always been respected members of society. He was steady, industrious, and never known to be intoxicated. Both brother and sister had always been on the best of terms."

Of Amalia Berri, the newspaper said she "enjoyed the esteem of the community.…She was kind and thoughtful of others and full of energy. Although the owner of a fine estate…she always attended to her drug store, with as much promptness as though she was just commencing business."

The *Warrenton Banner* reported that these were not the first fatal tragedies for the Berri and Hofius families. "We understand another [Hofius] brother committed suicide in Switzerland and a brother of Mr. Berri's met with a violent death in Germany."

The Berri Drug Store at 212 East High Street was purchased in 1872 by Dr. Nicholas DeWyl and Dr. Herman Bruns and continued as a pharmacy for another seventy years.

CHARLEY BROWN

IRISH QUARRY FOREMAN LOST LIFE FOR A QUARTER

A good deed and a misunderstanding led to the untimely death of one of the most skilled quarrymen in Central Missouri.

In 1878, the Kolkmeyer quarry between Harrison and Bolivar Streets north of Main Street was busy carving rock out for the railroad and city streets, which were both expanding rapidly.

Irish-born Charley Brown was foreman of the operation, which Henry Kolkmeyer had leased from the city beginning in May 1873. The quarry crew, about forty men, had made good progress into the bluff behind Captain Jefferson T. Rogers's impressive home facing the Missouri River.

One Sunday evening in June 1878, Brown found Irish shipbuilder John Maguire eating green apples on the railroad tracks near the quarry. Maguire was sick and looking for work. Brown invited Maguire to his home on McCarty Street between Bolivar Street and the Wear's Creek Bridge for a meal.

The Brown family offered him a bed until he could regain his strength. Mrs. Brown fixed meals and cared for Maguire the first few days. As his health improved, he began to chop wood for his board, dragging logs from the creek up to the house. Maguire had worked for the Pacific Railroad west to Kansas City and had been working odd jobs in an effort to return to St. Louis.

Later that week, the Browns hosted a dance at their home. At that time, Maguire first broached the topic of money with Charley Brown but could not get him to agree on a sum. At the end of a week, Mary Brown told her husband it was time for their guest to leave. That Sunday morning, Brown was sharing a drink at Herman Kolkmeyer's saloon with James Anderson when Maguire walked in to again discuss payment for his log-splitting. Brown invited Maguire to join them for a drink, which he refused impatiently. So Brown borrowed fifty cents from Mrs. Vaughn, who owned the store next to the saloon.

Then, in front of everyone in the saloon, Brown said, "Here is a man who has done some work around my house and I am going to make him a present of 50 cents."

Maguire took the change, walked away and then said, "My God, is this all you are going to give me for six days hard labor?" Brown answered, "Yes," because his wife had waited on Maguire while he was sick and accepted the inconvenience of having him in their home for a week.

After Brown left the saloon, Anderson asked Maguire about the situation. Maguire pulled out a horn-handled knife and shaved the hair of his wrist. When Anderson asked the price of the blade, Maguire replied, "This knife is worth two dollars for the business I intend to use it for."

Maguire returned to the Brown home, where he complained again about his compensation. The foreman ordered the stranger out of the family yard. Maguire went back to Kolkmeyer's saloon.

Albert Schroer met Maguire at about 5:00 p.m. on the Wear's Creek bridge, where the latter threatened to kill Brown if he did not pay him more. "This is the Irishman's rule to get satisfaction," Maguire said, showing Schroer the knife.

Schroer walked with Maguire toward Brown's house. At the same time, the Brown family had just returned from an afternoon visit to discover their well filled with large rocks. That's when Brown noticed Maguire coming their way. Charley Brown, followed by his wife, Mary, approached Maguire. While being asked if he had put the rocks in the well, Maguire plunged his knife between Brown's fifth and sixth ribs, across eight inches of his stomach. "Oh, I'm stabbed. Mary, I'm dead," Brown said.

Their oldest son, Charles A. Brown Jr., visiting from Scotland County, watched the terrible moment from the family's front porch. He grabbed his pistol from his trunk and headed toward Maguire. Brown Jr. fired at Maguire three times as the latter ran south on Bolivar Street toward the Franz Brewery, then fetched Dr. Alexander "Sandy" Davison. Later, Maguire lingered nearby, and Brown Jr. threw a brick at the villain but missed.

Quarry foreman Charley Brown made the fatal error of inviting a fellow Irish immigrant into his home on McCarty Street between Weir's Creek and Bolivar Street. *1869 Bird's Eye View.*

About the same time, William Rose was riding by from the Franz beer stand on McCarty Street. Brown Jr. told Rose what had happened and asked to borrow his horse. The rider refused but agreed to take the son's pistol and pursue Maguire. Rose caught up with Maguire at the Franz Brewery. When the rider told the slayer to surrender, Maguire drew out a bloody pocketknife and said, "If you take me, I'll stick this knife in you." The criminal turned and jumped across Weir's Creek, which Rose quickly crossed with his horse.

After shooting in the air, Rose nearly took Maguire prisoner. Again, Maguire drew his knife and ran away. He then met Brown Jr. and Henry Kolkmeyer, the latter subduing Maguire with a pistol handle to his head.

As Deputy Marshal Cohagan took Maguire to jail, the murderer was "defiant and unconcerned, as if nothing had happened, saying the jail wasn't fit for a white man to sleep in," the *State Journal* said.

The *St. Louis Globe-Democrat* described Maguire as "an Irishman with a thick brogue in his speech…of quick, nervous movements, and evidently of an excitable and morose disposition."

Maguire was found guilty of feloniously killing Brown by the coroner's inquest and found guilty of first-degree murder in January 1879. He was sentenced to hang but instead was given fifty years at the Missouri State Penitentiary. Eleven years later, Governor David Francis pardoned him.

PRIVATE JOHN WILCOX

EXECUTED FOR ANOTHER MAN'S BUSHWHACKING

A Miller County–born Confederate spy deserted the Sixth Missouri Cavalry CSA in General Sterling Price's army at Batesville, Arkansas, in the spring of 1864. On his way home to his widowed mother and four sisters—his father had been shot at Linn Creek by bushwhackers early in the war—he stopped at a barn dance in southwest Cole County.

Rebel John Peyton Wilcox, twenty, had already changed into civilian clothes but still held Confederate money, a revolver and a Union saber belt.

A Union squad of the Fourth Cavalry Missouri State Militia surrounded the barn on March 31, 1864, during a scouting mission. The soldiers assumed Wilcox to be a bushwhacker. Having served three years in the regular army, Wilcox assumed the Union soldiers were going to kill him, so he ran. That's when Lieutenant W.C. Lefevre shot him. The wound was at first thought to be fatal. Wilcox was taken prisoner and brought to the 230-bed U.S. General Hospital near the Capitol in Jefferson City under surgeon J.H. Ledlie.

After statements were taken in April from Wilcox, Lefevre and Sergeant James W. Chambers, Lieutenant Colonel Theodore Switzler, Central Missouri District provost marshal, ordered Wilcox "to be shot to death with musketry at Jefferson City, Missouri, as soon as he is sufficiently recovered to leave the hospital."

The matter was referred in May to the state provost marshal general, who said that Wilcox should be tried before a regularly organized court. Switzler added that he should be tried as a military insurgent and spy.

In June, Wilcox attempted an escape, stopping after four miles, when he was too weak to continue. A farmer returned him to the Union hospital. When he had recovered, Wilcox was held at the old Cole County Jail.

Meanwhile, Confederate guerrillas led by Wiley Shumate "rampaged, pillaged and murdered all over Miller County and the surrounding area" during the spring and summer of 1864.

Special Order No. 141 by Union brigadier general Egbert Brown at the district headquarters in Warrensburg was issued on July 1, 1864, because a "band of guerrillas, led by one Shumate, have committed depredations such as robbing and plundering peaceable, law-abiding citizens in Miller and adjoining counties."

Wilcox's fate lay in the last line of that order: "Upon the first overt act of lawlessness committed by this or any other band of guerrillas or bushwhackers upon the lives or property of the people of this district, the prisoner John Wilcox, a member of the said Shumates' band…will be immediately shot."

Having deserted at Batesville, Arkansas, on March 25, 1864, it would have been impossible for Wilcox to have joined Shumate's guerrillas, much less participate in any of their marauding, after crossing 230 miles in five days before his capture. Nevertheless, in August, Major General Alfred Pleasanton, district provost marshal, ordered the execution of Wilcox by Lieutenant Frank Swap, assistant provost marshal at Jefferson City. In the previous few weeks, the Shumate guerrillas had "committed many acts of murder, robbery and arson in Miller and Moniteau Counties."

In the days before his execution, Wilcox was visited by Reverend R.H. Manier of the Methodist Episcopal faith, former chaplain of the Forty-Eighth Illinois Volunteer Infantry and current chaplain of the Missouri State Senate and the Missouri State Penitentiary.

Before his execution, Wilcox was allowed to make a final statement. He said: "If I had had a fair trial, I could have proved that I never was a bushwhacker. I shall try to meet my fate as courageously as possible."

Just before 3:00 p.m. on August 12, 1864, John Wilcox was taken by wagon to the west-end scaffold built at Wear's Creek. His sister, Lucinda, rode with him as he sat blindfolded on his own coffin with his hands bound at his sides.

The first command to fire resulted in no wounds. A second firing squad was organized, and "twelve guns belched forth their deadly contents," the *Missouri State Times* reported. One ball passed through Wilcox's chin and five others into his breast.

Wilcox was seventeen when he joined the rebel cavalry of Colonel Benjamin Brown, who had been president of the Missouri State Senate, when the Missouri State Guard was organized by the Missouri General Assembly on May 14, 1861.

Brown's cavalry was at the Battle of Carthage on July 5, 1861, and the Battle of Wilson's Creek on August 10, 1861. Wilcox was wounded near Lebanon, possibly during the Union army's occupation in January 1862. After that, he was taken prisoner and made to take the oath of allegiance, which didn't last long.

Wilcox then enlisted with the CSA's Fourth Missouri Cavalry in August 1862. After arriving in Arkansas, he was reassigned to Burbridge's Regiment, which fought at the Skirmish of Cane Hill, Arkansas, on November 25, 1862. After that, he was "detailed on secret service duty" until he deserted.

Less than a year after his execution, Wilcox's sister Lucinda attempted to exact revenge on Union militia captain William Conner, whom she blamed for John's death. Conner was shot by two Miller County bushwhackers, whom Lucinda had hired. In retaliation, a former Union colonel caught the two assassins and murdered them the next year.

PART II

PROHIBITION

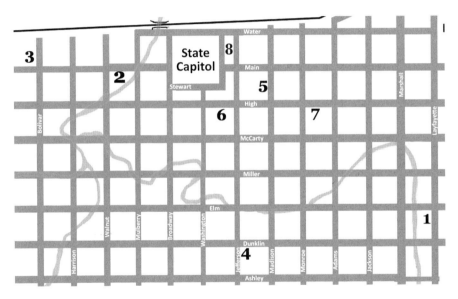

The following are estimated locations covered in Part II.

1. Lafayette Street District
2. Hildebrand soft drink parlor
3. Robben & Morgan soft drink parlor
4. Farmers Home saloon

5. Capital Tavern
6. The Smoke House
7. Alberthal boardinghouse
8. Schilling Home

Map credit: Stephen Brooks.

STILLS AND SOFT DRINK PARLORS, RAIDS AND REPEAT OFFENDERS

When the Eighteenth Amendment went into effect in January 1920, the question in Cole County wasn't if residents would comply, but where they would get their drinks.

The German-speaking population returned to the manufacture of home brew, and people of all heritages learned to build and operate stills. Those who were successful could satiate their own wants and make extra income during the Great Depression.

A few names continued to crop up in sheriffs' arrests and federal indictments for possession, sale or manufacture, even after serving time at the Cole County Jail or the federal prison at Leavenworth, Kansas.

Ford V8 Kept Him Safe

At least one local entrepreneur evaded arrest and fines while amassing considerable wealth. Paul Schmidt was the grandson of a pioneer blacksmith. A 1916 graduate of Jefferson City High School, Schmidt worked as a projectionist at the Capital Theater in the 100 block of East High Street.

Prohibition created the opportunity for him to operate a successful still operation until 1924, when he sold it to Fred Schilling. Schmidt diversified his revenue streams to include cockfighting, slot machines and gambling, according to Bob Kraus, who inherited Schmidt's paraphernalia. By 1928,

Right: Paul Schmidt was one of the successful bootleggers in Cole County. *Bob Kraus*.

Below: This 1925 Ford Lincoln could outrun any law enforcement of the day with its V8 engine, allowing Paul Schmidt to make his drops to St. Louis bootleggers at Mount Sterling. *Bob Kraus*.

the thirty-year-old Schmidt was able to buy his family blacksmith shop and two adjacent properties in the 300 block of Jefferson Street. A sharp-minded businessman, Schmidt invested his bootlegging revenue, converting the site to shops, including the city's first radio store, and modern apartments, which he designed.

When rye whiskey was cooking at the Algoa setup, the smoke could be seen seven miles up the Missouri River from the Missouri River bridge. The "pints" were filled to fourteen ounces and labeled with counterfeit medicinal alcohol labels.

In 1925, Schmidt focused on transportation, buying a 1925 Lincoln with an aluminum body and a V8 engine. The car, with the license plate number 986, was so fast that it could outrun any law enforcement vehicle in pursuit. He found safer business, providing liquor to St. Louis buyers at a drop-off near Mount Sterling.

When Prohibition was repealed in 1933, the car was retired under the apartment building. Schmidt went legit as the local Falstaff beer distributor for thirty years.

FISHERMAN TURNED STILL OWNER

Fred Schilling, to whom Schmidt sold his early still operation, became one of several who couldn't let the potentially lucrative work go, despite raids and jail time. Born in Ohio, Schilling had been known around town as a record-breaking fisherman before Prohibition. The World War I sailor's reputation for manufacturing liquor exceeded those outdoor accomplishments.

The largest still operation discovered up to May 1924 in Cole County and in the entire federal eastern district of Missouri was the one Schilling recently had purchased from Schmidt. Seven miles east of the city, dense woods hid the deliberately built facilities, and rural brush-burning disguised the cause of the smoke plumes.

Federal agents led by Gus Nations out of the St. Louis field office traveled on old St. Louis Road from the city onto new St. Louis Road. After crossing the Moreau River Bridge, they turned at a schoolhouse onto Robinson Ferry Road. Reaching a sign reading "Keep Out Private Property," the agents proceeded on foot.

The attendants of the facility somehow were alerted to the coming raid with just a few minutes to spare. Two parked cars had been left behind,

Most liquor manufacturing in Cole County took place on family farms and often could be disguised by burning brush. *Bob Kraus.*

one registered to Schilling's wife, and fresh tracks showed the workers fled on foot.

What the experienced dry agents found was a distillery capable of producing one hundred gallons a day at a value of $3,500. Items included three enormous hogsheads, five hundred gallons of working mash, a large copper still and coils, bottle materials and other liquor-making supplies. An advanced gas-powered water system operated two steam boilers.

The *Daily Capital News* called the site reminiscent of the Kentucky mountain moonshine dens. Agent J.C. Vaughan declared it the "largest and most complete he had ever seen." On closer inspection, Vaughan recognized the water tank, gas engine and boilers as those found a month earlier on the William Brenner farm near Algoa.

A frequent name in Jefferson City liquor sales and manufacturing during Prohibition, Fred Schilling had been arrested in that earlier raid on the Brenner farm, making moonshine instead of raising chickens, as his lease read. At the time of the massive raid off St. Louis Road, Schilling had been released on a $1,000 bond.

This time, agents didn't leave reusable materials behind. When "a sharp axe swung by a broad-shouldered man scarcely dented the massive copper construction," agents retrieved dynamite from town. It took three attempts, twenty sticks of dynamite and three barrels of coal oil to adequately break up the rig into "massive fragments."

The next month, June 1924, Agents Vaughan and Nations led another raid on a significantly sized distillery. Several other stills had been destroyed in recent weeks in the Tanner Bridge Road neighborhood. But the raiders anticipated that the operations would be quickly rebuilt and back in use.

So they watched and waited. When they learned that eight hundred pounds of sugar had been delivered on Tanner Bridge Road, the agents waited one more week, long enough for the manufacturing to begin. What they found on June 25, 1924, on Otto Tickelkamp's farm was "the most modern moonshine mill discovered" in the area. Agent John Pryor Jr. dubbed it a "1925 model." Instead of one cap and one worm for the vapor to pass through, this massive setup had five outlets, five oil burners and two monster concrete vats. The agents also confiscated two thousand gallons of mash. When raiders arrived at Tickelkamp's door about breakfast time,

Stills like this one were often recovered during raids and used as evidence for prosecution. *Bob Kraus.*

he simply said: "Come on, I'll take you to it. I knew you would come sooner or later."

At the end of its fiscal year in June 1924, the federal district court had assessed more fines than ever before. And "due to the activities of the U.S. dry agents in Cole County during the past two months there are a large number of prohibition cases on the docket for the court here this fall," the *Daily Capital News* reported. Among those cases was that of Fred Schilling, who was sentenced to eighteen months at Fort Leavenworth.

While Fred was away at prison, youngsters impersonating federal raiders came to the Schilling home. Mrs. Schilling ran them off with a shotgun when she saw them heading out of the barn with pieces of copper. The next day, when she returned to her home, she found a great deal of the copper missing, which later was found at a local junkyard.

When Schilling was released from prison, the couple moved to Westphalia, where he worked as a game warden. In 1928, the Schillings returned to Cole County, operating a barbecue stand at the Osage River Bridge Inn. Within months, their new operation was raided. Despite liquor found in December 1928, it continued to operate.

The next year, Schilling bought four new Whippet sedans and partnered with Ernest Norwood to open the Whippet Taxi Service, based at the Schilling home at 112 Jefferson Street.

In April 1929, Schilling again was arrested for sale of whiskey and maintaining a nuisance at the inn's barbecue stand. Agents had entered the inn's eatery and ordered sandwiches. Then they asked if the establishment had "anything to go with the food." The operator went next door to the Ewing dance-hall bar and brought back several bottles of beer. The agents drank the beer with their meal before making the arrest.

Mrs. Schilling was arrested with her husband in November 1929 for having five gallons of whiskey at their little gray bungalow on Jefferson Street, "in the shadows of the Governor's Mansion." Their "resort" had been a favorite destination during the previous state legislative session.

They were among twenty-four people arrested at the time in Cole County on dry law violations, including Schilling's taxi service partner Norwood, who operated a soft drink parlor at 416 West Main Street, and Louis Mehmert.

In January 1930, Mehmert and Roy Stockman charged Schilling with first-degree robbery after a whiskey delivery went bad. Mehmert and Stockman had contracted with Schilling for two hundred gallons of whiskey. The pickup spot was at Idlehour, the picnic grove on the east side of Green Berry Bridge over the Moreau River. At about 10:00 p.m., they arrived and were attacked by hijackers. Luckily, they were left with only cuts and bruises.

Schilling, driving a car in front of them, was to act as a scout for Mehmert and Stockman following in a pickup truck. But when they reached Moreau Park, Schilling "stepped on the gas" and headed for the city.

When Mehmert and Stockman reached Idlehour, shots were fired. One bullet went through the door panel, causing Stockman to jump from the truck with his hands in the air. He was hit with a pistol, kicked, cuffed and told to bury his face in the snow, the *Post-Tribune* reported.

Mehmert stayed in the truck after the shots were fired, and he was slow to comply with the hijackers' demands, resulting in a severe beating followed by "the admonition that if he 'opened his face once more,' he would be killed."

The two victims were unable to recognize the three attackers, who kept flashlights in their faces. Then the attackers left the scene with the truck and booze.

Once left alone, Mehmert and Stockman went to a nearby farmhouse and called Sheriff Ben Prenger, who sent deputies to the scene and requested the police watch for the stolen truck. "The men are certain that Schilling arranged for the robbery and that he led them into the ambush," the newspaper said.

The truck was found empty the next morning three miles west of the city on Ten Mile Drive. The police and sheriff then raided Schilling's home with a warrant to look for evidence to connect him to the assault and robbery. He was not home, and Mrs. Schilling had no information about the criminal activity from the night before, though she was arrested for another whiskey possession. Investigators found a rifle, identified by Stockman and Mehmert as a tool in their beating.

Stockman and Mehmert were not prosecuted for violations of the Volstead Act, because they were state's witnesses in a more serious offense, according to Prosecuting Attorney Nike Sevier. Schilling denied involvement in the robbery, claiming he, too, had been double-crossed. Schilling said that when he arrived at the pickup location, one of the rumrunners boarded his car, shoved a pistol in his ribs and ordered him to head back to the city. That's where the rifle came from, Schilling said.

This was not the first case of a hijacking in Cole County. In one instance, William Farris was the leader of a hijack squad that captured a truck of whiskey after tying the driver to a tree. Farris was found guilty, sentenced to prison, released on bond and disappeared. Another time, a group posing as Prohibition agents raided a farm south of town, taking all the whiskey. More cases went unreported, the victims fearing self-incrimination.

For the charges of operating their resort and liquor possession, Schilling and his wife were indicted in February 1930. He was sentenced to three years at Leavenworth. She was fined fifty dollars. Their home and operation was padlocked. And yet, the Schillings still did not give up the liquor trade. In November 1932, they were among twenty-seven violators caught up in a federal raid of Cole and Osage Counties, when they were operating a joint, again, on the Cole County side of the Osage River Bridge.

Resort of Ill Repute

Schilling was neither the first nor last to provide alcoholic refreshments through the Osage River Bridge Inn. Ownership turned over, but the location and its reputation remained constant.

Located at the intersection of Highways 50 and 54 on the line between Cole and Osage Counties, the inn was known for its live music, dance floor and barbecue. Bands like Schell's Orchestra and the Footwarmers brought the music, and Wallace Lawson was the acclaimed barbecue man serving up mutton, chicken, beef and spare ribs.

The barroom was reminiscent of old bars, including the brass footrail. In addition to the liquor, slot machines of varying size and gaming tables with railings could be found. The dance floor walls were lined with tables, and a player piano sat in one corner. The dance hall, cooled with electric fans, was one of the largest and finest country dance halls in Central Missouri, accommodating two hundred couples. Some called the place a "notorious and wide-open liquor and gambling resort."

By July 1928, the place had fallen into the hands of suspected Illinois mobsters who had been kicked out of Jefferson City. Bartender Raymond Burns and owner Eber "Slick" Ewing were arrested after ten gallons of alcohol, 250 pints of beer and a quantity of gin, whiskey and wine were found in iced receptacles.

Before buying the inn, Ewing had operated a place on Water Street in Jefferson City that was shut down by law enforcement. After the raid on the Osage River resort, he returned to 220 Water Street, where he and his wife, Maud, operated a "booze joint and house of ill repute."

Sheriff Ben Prenger led a raiding party in February 1929 that resulted in the arrest of four women and three men, as well as the seizure of eleven cases of home brew beer and another forty gallons in the making. "The daylight raid, which came as a big surprise to 'Slick' and his aides, cleaned up what has long been a disreputable resort in this city," the *Daily Capital News* reported. Law enforcement gave the operators the option to "leave the city and never return," the paper said.

With Ewing out of the area, Jefferson City resident Ernst Caton leased the Osage River Bridge Inn, planning to make it an orderly and up-to-date pleasure resort. He made a complete renovation of the main building and dance hall. Caton assured "the public that the lawlessness which has existed at the place in past years will not be permitted while he is in charge."

However, just a year after the raid on Burns and Ewing, Kansas City dry agents found plenty of violations at Caton's resort in July 1929. Although the place was empty when agents arrived, they waited long enough for the new owner and Anton Cremer to return with seventy-two pints of home brew in their car.

OTHER STILLS

Likely the most surprising still was the one making mash in a vacant room of the Executive Mansion basement. When the press contacted Governor Arthur Hyde, who was out of town, he denied the reports. Later, it was reported to be the property of a convict working at the residence.

Another of the largest stills known to be raided in Central Missouri was owned by William Weavers in December 1925. The Weavers farm was six miles southeast of Jefferson City on Bald Hill Road. Complaints had been made about manufacturing on the Weavers place for nearly two years, but it took that long to get a buy made by a county official to legitimize a warrant.

The raiding party, Sheriff Louis Withaup and his Four Horsemen, found a 150-gallon-capacity still with four burners in a fourteen-by-twenty-eight-foot building located fifty feet from the house. The setup even included a concrete cooling vat in an adjacent room. They also seized 20 gallons of whiskey, twenty-five barrels of mash, four sacks of sugar, several sacks of corn, two funnels, a tester and twelve feet of coil. The mash was destroyed, but the still and final products were brought back to Jefferson City as evidence.

In addition to being the largest raid at the time, Weavers' charges also were the first by Prosecuting Attorney Sam Haley under the Possession Act of 1923, which provided a straight penalty of two years at the Missouri State Penitentiary. "I'm gunning for the man higher up…the person who deliberately and for a profit manufacturers moonshine whiskey, often in such conditions of filth that the maker has no assurances that his next batch will not be poison instead of liquor," Haley said. He had heard "many complaints of late that manufacturers of whiskey are escaping with too small penalty.…I propose, if the juries will back me up, to make [moonshining] an unprofitable business."

Ultimately, Weavers, who operated a service station at Benton and McCarty Streets, was fined just $1,000.

Robbed and Raided

Like the Schillings, many people made their homes into liquor oases for those who could find them. These home-based businesses rivaled the saloons that were turned into soft drink parlors to keep afloat during the dry spell.

Sterling Burkett and Floyd Wiggins had the unfortunate timing to be robbed and then raided within twelve hours in May 1926. Burkett leased a section of the R.R. Robinett farm, south of Riverview Cemetery. From there, two kegs of whiskey had been removed one night. In the morning, the pair were dumbfounded, trying to ascertain their loss, when the sheriff and deputies pulled up.

Burkett told the sheriff that someone had stolen two ten-gallon jugs of liquor from his place the day before, but he told the sheriff he wished they had taken it all.

In December 1927, a booze party at Wiggins's home, at 406 West Atchison Street, turned bloody. A couple of men from Taos came to town to get drunk and visited several resorts before landing at the Wiggins home. Former highway worker Roy Barnett wanted to start a dice game, but Wiggins said he did not permit gambling. Barnett persisted, and an ex-convict neighbor, Joe Ford, argued.

When Barnett punched Ford in the eye, knocking him to the ground, Ford leaped to his feet, knife in hand. Taos blacksmith Lon Busker was stabbed in the leg trying to break up the row, and Wiggins was stabbed in the hand. Eventually, Barnett slugged his way out of the house, leaving his hat and coat behind and collapsing in front of Moerschel Products on Dunklin Street.

Although Jefferson City's alcohol underground never reached the level of violence of Chicago or other larger cities, sellers and makers could be territorial and certainly protective of their ventures. Suspecting that Edward Francis had tipped off law enforcement about his operation, Wiggins set a trap for the Hudson Essex agency employee to come by Wiggins's mule barn in the Mill Bottom.

As soon as Francis attempted to get out of the car, Wiggins struck him in the head with a revolver. Francis then threw a punch that knocked Wiggins down. At that, Wiggins's friends jumped Francis, giving him a severe beating. They then took to the car, breaking window panes and slashing the seats.

Not long after that, Wiggins moved to rural Boone County to help his younger brother Raymond grow a fruit farm. But after his brother committed suicide, Wiggins returned to Jefferson City and to his trade in alcohol. Six months after his brother's death, Wiggins, then twenty-nine and the father of three, pled guilty to the sale of whiskey and was sentenced to one year at the reformatory in Chillicothe, where the 1930 U.S. Census listed his occupation as "bootlegger."

Conrad "Coonie" George Hildebrand

Growing up in the Mill Bottom, Wiggins clerked for Conrad "Coonie" Hildebrand and later was bartender at the soft drink parlor at 411 West Main Street, next door to Henry Natsch's barbershop.

Hildebrand had been a city policeman for at least a decade until he was "dismissed for the good of the service" by Chief Frank Gretlein in August 1920. At the time, he had been assistant police chief and was being considered to replace Gretlein.

The Robben & Morgan soft drink parlor occupied the northwest corner of Bolivar and Main Streets, today Paddy Malone's. There, Hildebrand got drunk and assaulted Cole Junction youth Warren Smith. The matter moved out to the street, where Hildebrand, the primary witness, charged Smith with disorderly conduct. Later, it came out that Hildebrand had delivered whiskey to the Smith home and had been paid for it.

While liquor may have been the cause of Hildebrand's job loss, it also presented his second career. Wiggins was working for Hildebrand during the 1925 undercover operations by G.H. Foree at his West Main soft drink parlor.

This particular raid of both Hildebrand and Robben & Morgan was the result of a complaint filed by Henry Scheppers, who had just moved next door to the latter parlor. A Missouri Pacific roundhouse machinist, Scheppers claimed to have bought a half-pint from Hildebrand and another from John B. King at the West End Soft Drink Parlor, operated by George Robben and Eddie Morgan.

Scheppers said he filed the complaints "because of the great harm whiskey was doing to others and himself and that he desired to help clean up the town.…[He even] favored buying some dynamite and blowing them into smithereens."

After six months had passed and the court date arrived, Scheppers asked to retract his sworn statement, saying he "really could not remember just where he had obtained the liquor." A blacksmith used to owning his own shop, Scheppers moved out of the Richmond Hill neighborhood not long afterward.

The case against Hildebrand was dismissed for lack of a verdict. But a month later, Sheriff Withaup and his Four Horsemen were back for another raid, which sent Hildebrand to Leavenworth.

When Prohibition was repealed, Hildebrand operated a legitimate tavern.

West End Soft Drink Parlor

Perhaps no establishments were hit harder by Prohibition than the neighborhood saloon. Many closed their doors, like the Farmers Home on the South Side.

Other places existed as soft drink parlors, like that on the historic corner of Bolivar and West Main Streets. In 1873, Civil War veteran Nick Frank established the site, which has had many names over the years. The Richmond Hill city landmark today is Paddy Malone's. But during Prohibition, it was a soft drink parlor of questionable reputation.

Even before Prohibition, dry laws impacted this corner saloon, which hung a shingle reading "First Chance, Last Chance" after Callaway County voted itself dry and travelers across the 1896 Missouri River Bridge were faced with a choice. John Raithel owned the saloon until his death in 1907, and then it was operated by Joseph Meyers and George Robben prior to Prohibition.

The 700 West Main Street saloon closed in January 1920, when national Prohibition went into effect. It reopened as a soft drink parlor managed by John Russell and Charles Stampfli.

Under Russell and Stampfli, the location had a reputation for drunken people congregating and police raids finding evidence of Prohibition violations. Russell had the distinction of being the target of the first raid on a soft drink place by Jefferson City police in January 1922. What they found was a half-filled quart bottle of corn whiskey.

Nevertheless, complaints about the place, including "that women have frequented the place," led to an injunction suit. This "pretended soft drink parlor was a mere subterfuge and that he [Russell] has in fact for himself and his officers, agents, servants and employees openly and in violation of the laws of the state of Missouri and particularly of what is known as the prohibition law, engaged in storing for selling and disposing to the general public intoxicating liquors and beverages continuing alcohol in excess of one-half of one percent."

What today is Paddy Malone's was formerly a not-so-successful liquor operation disguised as a soft drink parlor during Prohibition. *Missouri State Archives, Ann Noe Collection.*

Furthermore, the newspaper said the "place was idle, lawless, turbulent, dissolute, [and filled with] immoral and dangerous persons addicted to ardent spirits which are a detriment to the morals of the community."

Stampfli, a paperhanger and plasterer, was a brakeman for Missouri Pacific Railroad before getting involved with the soft drink parlor business around the corner from where he grew up. Like his predecessor, only a half-pint of moonshine was found when the place was raided in June 1922.

George Robben and Eddie Morgan took over operations of the business about 1923 with bartender Fred Betts. The Robben & Morgan soft drink parlor first opened about 1921 at 607 West McCarty Street. Before that, Robben had his own pre-Prohibition saloon at 714 West Main Street.

Morgan had served as an alderman and was a leader in the State Federation of Labor. Robben was probably best known as a talented bowler and future manager of the St. Peter Church Alleys, which opened in January 1938.

The West End Soft Drink Parlor was frequently raided, and the owners, bartenders and employees were often charged with sale and possession of alcohol and maintaining a nuisance. Robben alone was arrested at least ten times throughout Prohibition. Eventually, the corner building was padlocked and later was used as an extension of Michael Sullivan's next-door bakery, then as a restaurant operated by Joseph Hammel.

Robben found a new location for his "nuisance" at 416 West Main Street. But it was his West McCarty Street home that was involved in perhaps the largest federal raid in Central Missouri. Eleven officials crossed three counties to bring in thirty-six liquor violators in November 1929.

"Jefferson City with its reputation of being wide open and wet as any city in the country is going to get dry," a federal official said. The agents had been in the area several months making buys from frequent violators like Robben, the Schillings and Weaver. Others caught in that raid were local grocer Tony Diemler, Wardsville farmer Anton Van Loo, Osage Bend farmer Theodore and Mary Mertens, Gladys Madison, Foot residents Fred and Emma Foster and James Dunnavant.

The courtroom the next day was so full that "all was confusion in federal court. Children with their parents cried. Wives were faint. Old men, who have lived in the county for years…appeared in the courtroom. It was the first time many of them had been in any kind of a court," the *Post-Tribune* reported.

And across the Capital City, "the drive was startling to the city and unexpected. Liquor prices shot skyward today and liquor was hard to find."

Unlike his previous dozen or so offenses, in which his charges were only minimal fines or dismissed altogether, Robben was sent to Leavenworth for two years following this 1929 raid.

FRED BETTS

One of Robben's former bartenders, Fred Betts, had his own share of raids by citizen-crusader Heber Nations and the feds. Before getting into the soft drink parlor racket, he and his brother Harry operated Jefferson Taxi Company out of 219 East Capitol Avenue.

Betts and Robben, along with Morgan, Joseph Kremer and W.C. Irwin, were called in for questioning in the conspiracy case against the Nations brothers and St. Louis's Griesedieck Brewery Company. "There were reports in circulation here last summer, which are said to have been well founded, that two or three cars of beer were shipped here and that the persons purchasing it were told it had 'protection' and there would be no trouble in handling it. Who promised the 'protection' at the time was never made known," the *Daily Capital News* reported.

Brothers Gus and Heber Nations were seen at most dry raids in Cole County in the first half of the Prohibition era. Note the axe mark on the still to the right. *Bob Kraus.*

Gus Nations left the federal dry agency, and Heber Nations resigned as the state labor commissioner. But neither admitted guilt in using their positions to enable Griesedieck to continue clandestine operations.

When KKK-endorsed Sheriff Louis Withaup took office in January 1925, Betts's place was his first raid. Betts's bartenders, William Burgett and Lester Dew, were sentenced to three months in the Cole County Jail for sale and possession.

In November 1930, Betts was part of a federal raid at a political rally prior to Election Day. Two homes on Elm Street near Washington School were hosting party meetings. Chief of Police Harry Parker had climbed onto the running board of Betts's car a few blocks before arriving at the meeting. Betts and Parker then walked toward one of the houses while three young people remained in the back seat.

Sol Monroe, a Black resident, opened the back door of the car and removed two bundles. At that point, the waiting federal agents arrested Monroe and discovered jugs of whiskey in the bundles. The police chief was investigated for involvement or knowledge and was eventually cleared. Betts and Monroe were not.

The Capital Tavern was opened at 228 Madison Street after the Missouri Power and Light Company relocated. *Cole County Historical Society.*

Betts was caught up in an April 1931 federal raid that left the city dry. One man told the newspaper, "If you don't think the federals have dried up the town, try and buy a drink."

Betts was among the few liquor dealers who continued in the business after Prohibition ended. He managed the Jefferson Buffet at 222 Jefferson Street and then operated the Capital Tavern at 228 Madison Street after the Missouri Power and Light Company moved out and Kemp Asel remodeled the building.

There, in January 1937, Betts shot Bill Woehrman. Apparently, they were leaders of rival gambling gangs. Scores of slot machines that had operated openly for the previous few months went immediately into hiding. In the end, Betts was found not guilty of murder on self-defense.

However, he had to file bankruptcy and sell the Capital Tavern the following November. In the spring of 1938, he held a formal grand opening for the Senate Lounge at 222 Madison Street. Here, Betts upped his game from sneaking bottles behind a soft drink counter to a place "smartly furnished and appointed, [that] radiates atmosphere of good fellowship and friendliness, [with a] modern bar [and] roomy booths."

THE SMOKE HOUSE

In January 1925, Betts and Freddie Clark were in a confrontation with Sam Soble after a boxing match. Soble was known for organizing, promoting and refereeing wrestling and boxing matches in the area. At the Midway Café following one of Soble's events, he threatened Betts and Clark with a revolver. Soble had several violent acts and cover-ups to his name.

Among Soble's many entrepreneurial ventures was purchasing the Smoke House. One block from the Capitol's south entrance, the location was the Hub Saloon by 1906, and later, 133 West High Street was converted into the Red Smoke House for billiards and cigars. The United Shoe Shining Shop took over before August 1924, when local entrepreneurs Herman and Mike McKinney renovated it, selling fresh candies and a full line of tobacco next door to an elegant shoeshine parlor.

By 1925, rising young businessman Paul Eveler had bought the property, where the U.S. Post Office is today. He leased the operations as the Capitol Smoke House to Soble and Cotton Meyers, who dropped the candy and added a barbershop.

A raid at the Smoke House in December that year confiscated ninety-four little bottles of whiskey in a satchel and fourteen pints. Black porter William Burgett was attempting to stash the hooch under the floor when deputies caught him. Soble and Burgett were fined $200 each for possession. Soble bought the Smoke House from Eveler in mid-1926, and he also acquired a Ten Mile Drive roadhouse, formerly a soft drink parlor operated by Betts.

Soble gave the rural place to Jack Stacey, a lightweight pugilist who was training for fights with Pewee Kaiser and Paul Stedman. They planned to make a training gym out of the place. A former employee, Clifford Kitchen, made good on a threat that he would get even with Soble by "telling the sheriff a few things."

When the sheriff's office made its raid in December 1926, the quantity of liquor found was "not enough for a decent drink," yet Stacey was fined $200. Although officials had the place long under suspicion, because it "radiated hospitality" and was "frankly lighted, so open and inviting, that it resembled no other 'farmhouse' in the county," the sheriff agreed it had been a frame-up.

Besides, "if the roadhouse had been in the habit of dispensing whiskey, the owners would have been amply warned" of the raid, officials admitted.

Two months later, Soble was arrested for operating a gambling joint on Madison Street. And then the grand jury ordered him to close the Smoke

House, which he agreed to do. Betts later reopened the corner as the Athletic Smoke House for a time. He was robbed of $1,000 in cash by St. Louis gangsters in August 1928, though he denied it and declined to report it.

In April 1928, Soble opened the Falstaff Sandwich Shop in the Ott Building, 113 West High Street, where his advertising said Falstaff beer would be served on draft. That October, he was arrested by federal agents again for violating the Volstead Act and sentenced to seventy-five days in the Cole County Jail, where he was "unanimously elected judge of the 'Kangaroo Court,' where he presided over merriment and a barn dance."

A year later, prosecuting attorney Sevier closed the Falstaff site, "because the shop has been noted as a rendezvous for undesirable characters" and because it was a disgrace to have it beneath the Capitol dome and across the street from the federal building. Sevier also suggested the shop had been the hangout for out-of-town gangsters.

"These places have been singularly free from serious raids and doubtless the parties running them had come to the conclusion that they were immune from any official interference," Sevier said.

"HABITUAL BOOTLEGGER"

Just as retail spaces and still shacks were repeatedly raided and reopened, bootleggers found it hard to let go of the easy money, if you could hide from the police.

One repeat bootlegger was Harry Wier, who had been a salesman and hotel manager before Prohibition, when he opened a soft drink parlor at 622 West Main Street. By 1924, he was living at 312 East Water Street, across from the Missouri Pacific depot. The first raid of his house uncovered a few gallons of moonshine in a piano box, and the second found twenty bottles of home brew and a gallon of a "mysterious concoction."

Wier was sentenced to three months in the Cole County Jail in November 1924. Four days later, he was driving a Buick Roadster on West Elm Street when he struck and killed a sixty-five-year-old deaf woman. Early reports said Mary McMullin stepped into his path while attempting to cross the street. However, a bruise to her hip indicated that she had been struck from behind.

By December 1925, Wier was bootlegging again. A raid discovered twenty-four gallons of whiskey, most buried under a "suspicious mound of

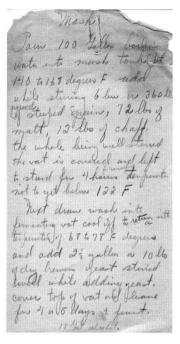

Bootleggers needed recipes, like this one for mash. Not producing correctly could result in blindness or death for consumers. *Bob Kraus.*

earth" in the backyard. He pled guilty again and was given three months in jail, again.

The *Jefferson City Post-Tribune* went so far as to dub him "king of the pocket bootleggers in this city" for several seasons. Prosecuting Attorney Haley added after Wier's third sentencing that Wier "has been a source of annoyance to the county authorities for months. One jail term or a prison term will never prevent the man from trafficking in moonshine liquor. He is a habitual bootlegger."

Three months into a year's jail time, Wier was granted clemency if he promised never to return to Jefferson City. He transferred his bootlegging activities to Sedalia, where, in March 1928, he pled guilty to the sale of whiskey and spent three months in the Pettis County Jail.

Breaking his word to not return, in August 1929, Wier was spotted and arrested, and he served out the remaining nine months of his previous Cole County sentence. Three months after his release, Wier shot himself behind Cleveland's Grocery on Mulberry Street.

HOME SALES

World War I sailor Fred H. Alberthal and his wife also established quite the sales reputation by the end of Prohibition. The morning of the circus parade in September 1925, Sheriff Withaup and his horsemen raided the Alberthal boardinghouse at 319 East High Street, seizing a jug of whiskey from behind the kitchen door. Fred was at work as a boilermaker. His wife, Emily Alberthal, began to weep.

Her husband had just received bond after a federal raiding party had found forty-eight pints in their home, charging him with possession, sale and maintaining a public nuisance. So, Emily Alberthal claimed this jug as her own. Many wives took the judgment for liquor running, especially after their husbands had been convicted multiple times.

The Alberthals managed to continue their business with mostly small fines for their persistent violations. Then, in July 1926, they were caught up in a four-location raid one weekend by Sheriff Withaup and his horsemen, which yielded in total five hundred bottles of booze. The next day's newspaper reported: "A blind man could have found his way to Sheriff Withaup's office on the second floor of the courthouse yesterday. The odor of whiskey and beer, taken in raids by the sheriff over the weekend, floated out into the corridors."

Someone had tipped off Alberthal, but he didn't quite get his stash moved before the raiders appeared at his Swift's Highway home. Alberthal was literally caught in the act of transferring beer from his home into his car. When Emily Alberthal did not answer the front door, Deputy Walter Withaup walked around to a window and saw her taking bottles out of the icebox and destroying them.

Again, Emily Alberthal assumed responsibility and took the possession charge. The total haul from this raid on the Alberthals was 186 pints of beer, 24 quarts of beer, one capper, one syphon hose and empty gallon- and half-pint containers.

Before a 1929 raid, federal dry officers in St. Louis had heard complaints that "whiskey was 'running like water' in the Capital City during the legislature session."

Emily Alberthal's boardinghouse was caught up in more than just booze in October 1929. Two married women who had come to Jefferson City to visit their brother at the Missouri State Penitentiary were invited by a local waitress to the Alberthal "resort," now at 1009 East Dunklin Street, for booze and a good time. The ladies were making merry, playing slot machines and enjoying an occasional drink purchased by the men who were there.

Then, the night turned, and one of the men got rough and tried to drag one of the girls from the house for a "moonlight drive." She showed her disinterest by kicking, biting, screaming and slamming a slipper against him. The tumult lasted so long that police arrived while they were still fighting outside. Of course, those inside the house fled in a hurry.

THE CAPITOL KU KLUX KLAN

FIERY CROSSES, CONFUSING DONATIONS

The issue of prohibition opened a new chapter for the Ku Klux Klan across the nation, promoting law enforcement as part of its anti-immigrant tenet. Missouri and the Capital City were not immune to this second wave of KKK activity.

The earliest accounts of the Klan in Jefferson City date to the summer of 1923, which followed the Columbia lynching of James T. Scott in April.

"Attempts to discredit the Klan only made it stronger. As has been noted by several historians of the 1920s Klan, the publicity given to the Klan…brought even more recruits into the Invisible Empire," historian Sean Rost wrote in "A Call to Citizenship: Anti-Klan Activism in Missouri, 1921–1928."

The first signs of the Ku Klux Klan's infiltration of Jefferson City followed a Monday night meeting in August 1923, when hundreds of men poured onto High Street from the Merchants Bank building, where their meeting was held. The next night, a fiery cross was set up at the corner of Chestnut and Elm Streets, where a "house of ill fame" operated. Although the Jefferson City Klan never claimed responsibility, most assumed it was them.

The third night, August 22, 1923, another cross was set afire on the WOS radio tower on the Capitol building. The following night, a third fiery cross was lit on Ten Mile Drive at the turnoff for what was known as the Chicken Dinner Club. It was suspected that gangsters were operating out of the local roadhouses. And the Chicken Dinner Club had a reputation for illegal liquor. That same night, an unexplained shooting took place as well.

The Merchants Bank building held meeting rooms in its upper stories, including the one used by the local Ku Klux Klan group in the 1920s. *Cole County Historical Society.*

On Friday, August 24, a fourth, though smaller, cross was set ablaze on the northwest corner of the Cole County Courthouse yard. Black businessman Robert Stokes, who owned the New Moon Hotel across Commercial Way from the courthouse, saw the light flash but was not fast enough to see who lit it.

"No words of warning were placed near…the crosses…but it is believed to be the purpose of the Klan to call attention to the fact that they are now organized locally," the *Russellville Rustler* reported.

At the first signs of the organizing of the Ku Klux Klan in Jefferson City, the *Democrat-Tribune* printed an editorial: "Should a group of persons hiding their personality behind hoods and masks take upon themselves the duties of the civil authorities, it would be anarchy.…To break one law to uphold another is not the proper way to build a successful city."

Joseph Goldman, editor of the *Jefferson City Tribune*, was a strong opponent to the presence of a Ku Klux Klan chapter in the Capital City. *Cole County Historical Society.*

In response, the Jefferson City Klan printed a full-page ad in the *Democrat-Tribune*, saying, "our hostility to bootleggers, professional gamblers and all forms of organized and commercial lawlessness or vice is unlimited. We will spare no effort, time or expense to uproot these things and drive them from the community."

The ad went on: "There is not agitation in this order, nor in the hearts of its members, toward the Jew, Negroes or the Roman Catholic Church...regardless of any reports that you may have received from the organization's enemies." However, among the cardinal principles listed in the ad, the first two were "Tenets of the Christian Religion" and "White Supremacy," and number fourteen was "Limitation of foreign immigration."

As weeks passed after the initial show of presence, Joseph Goldman, who was editor of the *Jefferson City Democrat-Tribune* at the time, provided a consistent print opposition to the growing Klan. "I am against this organization, not because I am a Jew, but because I believe first in the government of the United States."

Of course, the local Klan benefited from its Exalted Cyclops Heber Nations, who happened to be editor of the *Jefferson City Daily Post*. Nations often accompanied his brother Gus, who was the head of the Kansas City dry raiders' office, on local raids.

The *Daily Post* office on Madison Street was among several locations that felt retaliation from the community, which was not welcoming of the Klan's activities. A carload of men fired revolvers into five business houses on High Street supposed to have been owned by Klansmen. The plate-glass windows were riddled with bullets, and the same was done to the *Daily Post*'s front window on the first Sunday in October 1923. Former newspaper owner Joseph Sailer was asleep upstairs and saw nothing. But Phil Berry, who would later become a sheriff's deputy, lived across the street and saw the flashes from the guns and the large car drive south on Madison Street.

The same night, gunmen visited two of the disreputable locations where fiery crosses had been posted just a few weeks earlier. Five shots went through the frame of the Chestnut Street bawdy house and more at the Chicken Dinner Club on the Cole Junction Road, off Ten Mile Drive.

"Jefferson City cannot be allowed to go wild and permit shooting at will," Prosecuting Attorney Sam Haley said.

Law enforcement presumed the Klan had done that as well, as another of its principles is "to protect the home and chastity of womanhood." They were unsure of the motive against the *Daily Post*, which had just published an editorial in favor of the Klan. But that edition also had a front-page editorial against "organized masked depredations."

"As a result of the organization of the Ku Klux Klan in this city, the once peaceful and progressive city has been torn asunder and business is slowly but surely becoming paralyzed," Goldman said in the *Democrat-Tribune*.

Former state senator and president of Central Missouri Trust Company Sam B. Cook feared Jefferson City would become a "wild west town" and urged support of law enforcement in solving the matter.

The Cole County Commission offered a $500 reward for the arrest and conviction of those responsible for the "malicious destruction of property through the lawless discharge of firearms." Mayor Cecil Thomas added $200. Thomas, nicknamed "The Builder," said: "Lawlessness and intimidation are the weapons of cowards and the perpetrators should be punished to the full extent of the law. If Jefferson City is to continue its steps forward, we must all join together, Protestant, Catholic and Jew…we must know no creed or no color, but work for the common good of the community."

The *Daily Capital News* followed with its own call to citizenship: "Jefferson City cannot permit its citizenship to be split and its future impaired because of the actions of hot heads and it behooves every safe and sane resident of the city to see that the fanatics do not tear down what it has taken generations to construct.…We must not be torn asunder like other places have been, but instead, must stand as one for good citizenship and for Jefferson City.… If there be a Ku Klux Klan here, and we believe there is, it behooves the leaders to live up to their claim of 100 per cent Americanism, which does not mean arraying friend against friend or sect against sect."

Local Klan activities outside their meeting hall cooled for a few months. But in February 1924, Missourians across the state were shocked to learn that hundreds of Klan members met in the newly completed Capitol's House of Representatives.

The speaker was Reverend Z.A. Harris of Blackwell, Oklahoma, who "discussed dangers of corroding American ideals of nationalism, should immigration not be sufficiently retarded to prevent an over-influx of the ideas of internationalism now flooding into the country from abroad," according to the *St. Louis Post-Dispatch*.

Neither the speaker nor his topic was as offensive as the fact that local Klan leaders Heber Nations, who was the State Labor Commissioner at the time, and Carroll Bailey had been given permission to use the statehouse from Harry Woodruff, commissioner of the Permanent Seat of Government.

It had been the local custom to allow public organizations to use the Capitol spaces when the Missouri General Assembly was not in session. Secretary of State Charles Becker defended the decision. "I have no prejudice against any organization or church. As long as an organization of any kind wants to hold an orderly, public meeting in the hall, no lines will be drawn."

The event had been openly and publicly advertised with handbills circulated across the city, including one posted to the door of St. Peter Church. Nations described the event as patriotic and scholarly with the "greatest crowd that ever jammed the legislative hall." But when the time came, the hall doors were locked and sentries posted when the meeting began.

Six months later, the local Klan began advertising another meeting in the House of Representatives. This time, the board of the Permanent Seat of Government passed a resolution prohibiting the use of the Capitol for secret or closed meetings.

"I do not agree with the Ku Klux Klan and no 100-percent American needs a secret organization to prove his right to that title," Governor Hyde said. About 260 official representatives from chapters across the state were turned away from the Capitol and sent instead to the local Klan chapter's meeting hall on the third floor of the Merchants Bank building.

By this time, Nations had estimated the local Klan's membership at one thousand. Local affairs were organized by Earl A. Kitchen, whose office was in the Central Missouri Trust Company Building.

DONATION DILEMMA

The local Klan created a shocking dilemma when a Black messenger delivered checks of twenty-five dollars each to the four Black churches meeting for Sunday night services in July 1924. The checks arrived with letters of goodwill, the *St. Louis Argus* reported. One read, "All good Negro citizens are 100 per cent American"; another read, "The Knights have the most kindly feeling and spirit of helpfulness for the colored race."

Second Baptist Church was one of two local Black churches to return the twenty-five-dollar donation made by the local Ku Klux Klan chapter. *Joyce (Logan) Webb.*

"Nothing has caused a greater stir among church people here than has this one act of the Klansmen. There seems to be some division among the members, as well as officers and ministers. Some express fear of violence, if the money is returned, while others say 'we cannot use it regardless of the cost,'" the *Argus* reported.

Quinn Chapel AME, under Pastor H.P. Greenlee, and Second Baptist Church, with Pastor Dr. E.L. Scruggs, declined to accept the donated "blood money" and each received a $100 check in the mail from an anti-KKK association from Joplin, complimenting the churches on their "dignified attitude" to refuse the money. "The negroes of the Baptist Church of Jefferson City are not for sale," said Reverend Virgil Goins, acting pastor of Second Baptist.

Zion AME Church pastor Paul Holley and Second Christian Church pastor John Wesley Damel accepted the donations to carry on their missions. The *Argus* called this "approval on the acts of the klan." The Black newspaper urged the congregations to override their ministers' decisions. "If a preacher is so ungodly as to be willing to accept money from the Klan, then we appeal to the officers of the church to act and act speedily, for such a preacher may

The local Ku Klux Klan chapter took advantage of the thousands of visitors at the 1924 Capitol dedication to advertise its largest local recruiting and induction event. *Missouri State Archives, Joseph Summers Collection.*

be properly called a traitor and a disgrace to the high calling of the Christian [*sic*] ministry," the *Argus* said.

A week later, the *Argus* attacked Damel personally, calling for him to be not only "unfrocked as a minister" but also removed as an instructor at Lincoln University. Neither happened, and Damel continued to serve the church, university and community, even having a building on campus named for him.

In the fall of 1924, the local Klan also made donations to some white churches. While a revival meeting was in progress at Spring Valley Church at Henley Lake, the sermon was interrupted when twenty-five hooded KKK members marched down the aisle and lined up in front of the pulpit. A Klan member delivered a brief address on the history and principles of the Klan, a donation was made and they withdrew. A week later at New Hope Church near Centertown, a similar visit and donation was made.

LARGEST KLAN GATHERING AT LAMPKIN SPRINGS

When the Missouri State Capitol was dedicated on October 6, 1924, the local Klan not only participated but also promoted its own upcoming event. And one of its leading members was among the day's dignitaries. Former state auditor John P. Gordon was chairman of the oratorical portion of the dedication. He tried to use his position to remove a depiction of Jesuit explorer Jacques Marquette from the major pageant reminiscing the state's history. Gordon also protested having Right Reverend John Joseph Glennon on the program. Even as he introduced the St. Louis archbishop to deliver the opening invocation, Gordon could do little more than mutter the Catholic official's title.

During Dedication Day, the local Klan, like dozens of local organizations, set up a food stand to help feed the thousands of single-day visitors. And it boldly posted flyers promoting its own barbecue a few days later.

More than one hundred cattle and sheep were barbecued for the rally at Lampkin Springs, three miles south of Jefferson City. Souvenir stands included little plaster Klansmen, Klan canes and pennants and large balloons. A plane with a burning cross attached to one of its wings flew over Jefferson City and nearby towns, and music concerts and lectures preceded the fireworks and initiation ceremonies.

JOHN P. GORDON

Auditor

State Auditor John P. Gordon was a vocal member of the Jefferson City Ku Klux Klan until he had a change of heart and became equally outspoken against the organization. *Missouri State Archives, 1913–1914 Official Manual.*

Politically, the local Klan began to split and lose its influence in November 1924, when members differed on candidates to be endorsed by the Klan, including future sheriff Louis Withaup. Later, Nations defended the small window of Klan presence, saying it had accomplished its mission of closing soft drink parlors and electing officials who would enforce the law.

Less than a year after the Capitol dedication, Gordon admitted: "I see no need for further existence of the Klan as now operated....I was led into the Klan by misrepresentation of its policies and purposes. Until I discovered its evil tendencies, I made no concealment of my membership in the organization. Now, since I have become convinced that its practices are opposed to good citizenship and good government, I shall, with equal frankness announce that I am no longer affiliated with the Ku Klux Klan.... Assisting in law enforcement has dwindled into a mere sideline, and the main efforts are devoted to playing small politics and dividing communities into warring factions."

SHERIFF LOUIS WITHAUP AND THE FOUR HORSEMEN

BREAKING LAWS TO ENFORCE THEM

The election of Louis Withaup as Cole County sheriff for the 1924 term was strongly attributed to the influence of the short-lived Ku Klux Klan presence.

A secret Klan meeting at the end of October 1923 endorsed Withaup. With 1,200 people attending at the local hall in the Merchants Bank building, cheers could be heard for blocks, and thunderous applause continued for five minutes when Withaup was announced the favorite, a local newspaper reported.

Withaup was a Democrat, but the local Klan expected its Republican members to cast their vote his way, too, despite Fred Hueller, who won the August Republican primary, also being a Klan member. This created a split in the local Klan chapter, spelling the beginning of the end of the Kapitol Klan's influence. The goal was to keep Felix Senevey, the anti-Klan Republican running as an independent, out of office.

Although the three-way contest for sheriff could have become a nasty political entanglement, Hueller neither pulled out of the race nor made a complaint. Senevey did his share of mudslinging. But it was the winner, Withaup, who showed himself to run a "clean and above board campaign." The *Daily Capital News* said he treated his opponents with friendliness and courtesy and answered questions on his campaign positions fearlessly and fairly.

Winning by 121 votes over Senevey, Withaup "pledged to the strict and impartial enforcement of the law," which would "sound the death knell of the bootlegger and gambler." He was the only Democrat to win office that term.

Withaup was not only the local Klan's preferred sheriff, he was also one of its "foremost members." Above the door of his business, Withaup Tire Repair Shop on Capitol Avenue, was the KKK's catchphrase, "100%." He was among the few who openly acknowledged membership. "Such courage was rare among the Kluxers and the 100 per cent sign is believed to have been responsible for his endorsement by the hooded gentry for sheriff," a newspaper later noted.

In addition to being a convenient "annex" for the sheriff's office to store the abundance of dismantled stills and other alcohol production–related evidence, Withaup's shop was a gathering place for the KKK.

During his four years, Withaup held true to his campaign promise to enforce the law. He worked on his own or with federal agents to make hundreds of arrests related to the Volstead Act. He spent his own money to secure buys, which the prosecutor required before issuing a warrant. And he made plenty of enemies.

Living up to his promise left him with few job prospects after he lost the 1928 election. Five years later, he took his own life.

Withaup was orphaned at age nine, learned the blacksmith trade in Warren County and opened his own shop in Jefferson City by 1895. By 1920, he had added tire repair to his old-fashioned trade at 209 East Capitol Avenue. Before being elected sheriff, he had been appointed fire chief by Mayor A.C. Shoup.

Withaup had a powerful physique and magnetic personality and was called "one of Cole County's most colorful characters" by the *Jefferson City Post-Tribune*. He was a "big-hearted jailer," leading to more than fair treatment of the men held in the county jail. Eventually, his benevolence led to federal charges of coddling the inmates.

Before that, however, Withaup substantially increased the number of liquor-related raids in Cole County. When he took office on January 1, 1925, Hueller was his first deputy appointee, along with Phil Berry. Just fifteen days after taking their oaths, the three new officers joined four federal Prohibition officials to raid several soft drink parlors in the city.

The take could have been even more impressive if not for an overzealous newspaper editor and political interference. *Daily Post* editor Heber Nations, who had been a predominant citizen-raider in previous years with his brother Gus, prematurely printed the locations of the raids, tipping off some of the places before the raiders could catch the liquor.

Withaup's zealous arrests were not always supported by the courts or local officials. Within an hour of this first raid, an unnamed, prominent man who had been caught in the roundup was released on the order of Mayor Cecil Thomas. The mayor further ordered any record of that man's arrest be destroyed, a courtesy he apparently extended many times in the past.

Another time, Withaup discovered liquor in the pocket of Osage County prosecuting attorney John Peters. But Judge Henry Westhues sustained a motion to suppress evidence and discharged the case. Some months later, two prominent Moniteau County men were transporting liquor from Osage City. Their car was searched near today's Apache Flats. When liquor was discovered, J.W. Longdon and Newt Birdsong made failed attempts to buy the deputies' silence in order to avoid publicity. Again, Withaup made the arrest, but again, Judge Westhues suppressed the evidence. Such actions left the community asking, "What's the use?"

Withaup held fast to his commitment. By July 1925, so much illegal alcohol had been amassed in Withaup's courthouse office as evidence that it had to be dumped out. The *Daily Capital News* described it: "The evidence which has been the cause of yearning and temptation around the courthouse for several months [was] poured into the basin while a number of witnesses, dry-tongued and sad, stood around."

The next month, Frank Moore, a former prizefighter, was arrested for driving while intoxicated six miles west of the city on California Road. He and his aged mother were taken to the sheriff's office to "sober up." Instead, Moore stole a half-pint of the evidence stored in the sheriff's office, asked to go to the washroom and "was in the middle of a lusty swig when the deputy sheriff stopped him."

Sheriff Withaup cracked down on stills and sales, as well as "orgies" and dances. In February 1925, his deputies hid in the brush outside a dance at the State Park, today's McClung Park, to catch young people drinking in the parking lot. But the officers were so far away that by the time they rushed the young couples passing around a bottle, the evidence had been locked away in a car.

It was an impossible task for law enforcement to keep up with the gatherings. In one month, janitors at the Capitol carried away nearly three hundred whiskey flasks, wine bottle, jugs and Mason jars. The Missouri General Assembly proposed a resolution to limit use of the Senate Lounge in the new Capitol. Speaker of the House Jones Parker said: "The people of

Jefferson City think they own this Capitol.…There is no reason that these chambers should be used by loafers and loungers."

The sheriff and his deputies were not limited to land in their raiding efforts. In January 1926, they confiscated a small houseboat anchored away from shore on the Osage River, eleven miles from the city, that held a still, whiskey mash and a distilling apparatus.

They often assisted in raids in adjacent counties, too. Once, in Callaway County, they nearly were blown up during the arrest of Dr. H.E. Johnson, who was wanted in Cole County for whiskey possession. The Black doctor was seated near a King heater, where he had hidden the whiskey. The lid flew from the stove as a crash and loud explosion revealed a blue flame reaching toward the ceiling.

The week before, the raiders had found five gallons of whiskey at the doctor's home. His office at 215½ Jefferson Street had already closed when the state board revoked his license. After that, Dr. Johnson was arrested, if not charged, several times with possession and manufacturing.

The Four Horsemen

Withaup's efforts caused the county to increase manpower. Judge Henry Westhues approved additional deputies, including the sheriff's son Walter Withaup and "Jinx" Coffelt. But Westhues did not approve prominent local Klan member Carroll Bailey, who often went on the raids as a citizen, as Heber Nations had.

The *Jefferson City Tribune* dubbed the sheriff, Phil Berry, Coffelt and Deputy Withaup "The Four Horsemen." Later, F.H. "Slim" McCullough joined them, and it became "the Sheriff and the Four Horsemen." During their reign, the Four Horsemen made more than one hundred liquor raids, with and without federal agents.

As much as Sheriff Withaup and his Four Horsemen elevated the level of law enforcement related to liquor in the Capital City, the sheriff's officers also brought their own elements of lawbreaking.

For example, John Jones was briefly appointed a deputy sheriff after being named watchman at the "new" high school, today's former Simonsen Ninth-Grade Center. But within a few months, Jones was found to be drunk and in possession of whiskey, leading to a rampage in which he was pursued by other deputies and city policemen. Once caught, Jones protested that he could not be arrested because he was an arresting power. So Withaup fired him; then they arrested Jones and took him to jail.

DEPUTY TURNED RUMRUNNER

Another short-term deputy, Jack Hess, who had been a special agent for Missouri Pacific Railroad, participated in a number of county and federal dry raids in Cole County. After leaving the Cole County sheriff's department, Hess took up bootlegging in Callaway County. He was never under suspicion until "he boasted that enforcement officials in Callaway County were a sleepy set and would never catch him transporting whiskey," the *Jefferson City Post-Tribune* reported. Taking that as a challenge, Callaway County sheriff's deputies sought out Hess at Auxvasse.

When Hess sped by at forty miles per hour, Deputy W.P. Garret stepped on the gas while Deputy J.C. Owen stood on the running board firing shots in the air. After a ten-mile pursuit, Hess pulled onto a side road and took off on foot. The Callaway officers opened fire, hitting a finger on his right hand and then a second finger on his left. When Hess was apprehended, the officers found thirty-six pints and one gallon of whiskey in the car. Hess said that after losing his job in law enforcement, he was unable to find decent employment, causing him to resort to running whiskey.

JAMES "PHIL" BERRY

One of the rogue Four Horsemen was James "Phil" Berry. The Spring Garden–born farmer had previously served as justice of the peace for Hickory Hill.

In August 1925, Deputy Berry struck an Osage City farmer while he was in custody. Herman Schmidt had been arrested by Deputy Withaup after highway department official Esthus Crutcher complained that Schmidt had sped through a barricade on St. Louis Road and almost ran him over. Schmidt had brought his wife and baby to town to see a doctor. The arrest kept them from that appointment.

As the Schmidt family sat in the sheriff's office for some time, Schmidt "was indignant and greatly excited over his arrest." Eventually, Schmidt announced that he was going home with his family. Deputy Berry told him to remain seated, but Schmidt ignored him, talking loudly and protesting his arrest. At that point, Berry pushed Schmidt back into a chair, but Schmidt rose again in protest. Berry said he then "had reason to believe Schmidt was about to strike him when [Berry] whipped out his revolver and struck [Schmidt]," one newspaper reported.

Another newspaper reported that the farmer was holding his baby at the time. The officer's blow to the head knocked Schmidt against a desk and rendered him partially unconscious, and Berry then kicked him twice. Schmidt was left with a scalp wound that covered his face with blood.

Just two months after the Schmidt incident, Berry shot inmate Henry Spencer, who was climbing down a bedsheet rope in an escape attempt from the old county jail. After being shot down, Spencer said he was brutally kicked and cursed by the deputy. Spencer alleged that he was "maliciously, unlawfully, brutally, oppressively, without cause, justification and provocation, without warning and without given a chance to surrender, brutally shot by [the] deputy."

Both cases appeared in the May 1926 term of the Cole County Circuit Court, which was standing-room-only, filled mostly by farmers. The jury sided with Schmidt, but the judge dismissed the Spencer case. Berry then lost his job.

CHRISTOPHER COLUMBUS "JINKS" COFFELT

At the same time that Berry was dismissed from the sheriff's department, Christopher Columbus "Jinks" Coffelt was suspended, pending his own appearance in court. The farmer from Scruggs Station had served with Berry in the Missouri National Guard Second Infantry in federal service from June to October 1916 during the Mexican border crisis. Before joining the Four Horsemen, Coffelt was a city fireman and a storekeeper at R. Dallmeyer Dry Goods.

In March 1926, Deputy Coffelt "staged a one-man raid at Nick Kielman's Farmers Home." Among the sixteen South Side pinochle players gathered around the table at 10:00 p.m. were a well-known grocer, a county judge, a bank cashier and a respected veteran. When Coffelt saw the chips on the table, he told the men to put their cards down. Richmond Hill grocer Emil Graessle took him for a bum and refused, because he held a good hand.

The ECCO Lounge originally was Farmers Home saloon. During Prohibition, owner Nick Kielman opened the room for friendly card games. *Sue Ferber*.

Graessle "told Coffelt to go to infernal regions." When Coffelt pulled out his revolver, Graessle complied.

The off-duty deputy then called Sheriff Withaup, who arrived on the scene, assessed the situation and then said to his deputy, "Come on Jinks, let's go." Coffelt later said that he made the raid because a woman complained her husband was losing money playing cards there.

When the Volstead Act went into effect, Kielman was forced to close the saloon. He stayed in business with the hotel, which catered to out-of-town farmers, with a pool hall and a barbershop. But Kielman kept the saloon, today ECCO Lounge, open as a club room for friends. The South Side pinochle games had been going on for years.

The day after Coffelt's "raid," he was charged with disturbing the peace and drawing his weapon. A *Jefferson City Tribune* editorial jested, "About the only indoor sport that's left now on cold, inclement winter nights is thumb-twiddling or reading."

Coffelt was found guilty of disturbing the peace by a jury in a "trial full of humorous situations....The audience was kept in a continuous uproar and Jinx himself could not restrain his laughter, when the witnesses told of his antics on the night of the memorable raid," the *Tribune* reported. He also had been charged with disorderly conduct for being drunk, but on a change of venue the case was discharged when the jury could not agree.

Although suspended as a deputy, Coffelt continued participating in the liquor raids. After a federal raiding party found a still in operation in Osage County in April 1926, orders were given to set fire to the shack and moonshine paraphernalia. Coffelt tied a sack soaked in fuel to a stick, lit it with a match and torched the inside of the shack, resulting in an explosion and a flame scorching Coffelt's face and arms, as well as slightly burning Deputy "Slim" McCullough.

Before he left the sheriff's department, Coffelt also wound up in fisticuffs in the Cole County courtroom. Local attorney Nike Sevier and Deputy Coffelt "by and with the consent of the prosecuting attorney who promised immunity from prosecuting and with court in recess for the occasion… fought it out on the concrete floor of Justice Leslie's court."

Coffelt had been the first witness for the state in a case against young partiers at State Park. Sevier called Coffelt a liar when the latter said he could identify the man from fifty feet away in the dark. Coffelt then said, "You can't call me a liar. You're just another." That's when prosecuting attorney Sam Haley suggested "that's fighting language," and the judge agreed.

Sevier pulled off his coat, and he and Coffelt squared off inside the space created by the crowd. Deputy Berry rushed in to stop the nonsense, but Withaup and Haley both stopped him. The *Jefferson City Tribune* gave a blow-by-blow account of the poorly contested wrestling match, which resulted in a draw.

Then the two fighters returned to exactly where they had left off, with Coffelt on the witness stand and Sevier asking questions. "Haley seemed to enjoy the spectacle. He said that when men so far forget themselves to use language of that kind, the court might as well recess long enough to permit them to fight it out," the newspaper reported.

Sheriff Withaup himself was later involved in a courtroom altercation. Toward the end of his tenure, while on the witness stand, he was slapped by local attorney H.P. Lauf. Although Withaup rose in anger, he did not strike back. Nonetheless, Judge Henry Westhues reprimanded Withaup, not Lauf, saying, "An officer of the court should know how to conduct himself." Lauf had been trying to compel the sheriff to turn over a diamond ring valued at $1,500 that had been given to him by a former inmate. Lauf charged that an item of such value was presumed to be a bribe, to which Withaup had called the attorney a "—— liar."

INSIDE THE JAIL

On the trail of lawbreakers, Withaup was persistent. However, once they were behind bars, he seems to have been a little too nice.

As was common in county sheriff's offices of the day, the sheriff and his wife, Augusta (Schaberg), moved into the sheriff's residence, provided by the county, adjacent to the jail. Augusta Withaup was expected to prepare the inmates' meals and to keep an eye on things when the sheriff was away. Appointing their son Walter as a deputy was a convenience.

Most minor offenders were given a $100 fine or thirty days in jail. Often, the latter was chosen. In 1925, the county's jail costs reached $4,000, so the court was "trying to devise a means to work the prisoners and make jail less attractive." Judge Leslie said: "Many of the prisoners are glad to receive a jail sentence, which will keep them warm and dry and well fed during the winter months….They like nothing better….Find some means of making jail life less attractive, create a rock pile or put the men at work that will help in paying for their keep, there would be more dissatisfaction."

The two-story stone Cole County Jail, built in 1842, sat at the southeast corner of McCarty and Monroe Streets, where the veterans' memorial is today. *Library of Congress.*

Withaup's hospitality became a federal crime in 1927. Several federal prisoners from Kansas City were sent to the Cole County Jail to serve their sentences for liquor law violations in 1925–26. As of December 1924, the federal government had to pay fifteen dollars per month for the use of the county jail, the same as the city. Before that, the county covered the housing costs, except for sixty cents per day to feed federal inmates.

In this instance, Federal Marshal I.K. Parshall told Withaup that the inmates he brought from Kansas City were "nice fellows, high-class men" and should be treated well. So, at least seven of the criminals were set up in three rooms on the second floor of the sheriff's residence. These "good fellows, druggists and former saloon keepers, well-known around Kansas City" paid to furnish their quarters comfortably and hired another Kansas City federal prisoner, Bob McDonald, to be their cook and butler.

Withaup was charged in federal court for allowing too many liberties to these and other inmates. Allegations included that they were allowed to leave the sheriff's residence unguarded. Withaup did admit that the prisoners were allowed to stroll the local business district accompanied by a guard. Found guilty, Withaup's sentence was reduced in December 1927 to a $500 fine and thirty days in the Jackson County Jail. The sentence was suspended.

PART III

ESCAPES

THE WALLS

HOW TO FLEE THE MISSOURI STATE PENITENTIARY

For the community around the walls, the greatest concern was for their own personal safety. Nothing threatened that more than escapes, which were all too frequent during the Missouri State Penitentiary's first century.

Escape attempts in several instances resulted in death for community residents or their family members employed at the prison. At other times, desperate men reverted to their old vices of drinking, violence and poor decisions. In the first sixty-five years of the Missouri State Penitentiary, 583 escapes were successful.

Early on, the prison was not operated by the state but by local businessmen who were trying to make the prison profitable. Therefore, they often sent inmates to work labor projects, for which the prison was paid. But they also used low numbers of untrained staff to oversee the criminals. And little of the private investors' money was spent on the inmates, who wore threadbare clothes, ate worm-filled meals and lived in inhumane conditions.

Several times, the town and its state representatives tried to end the use of inmate labor outside the walls, but the need for businessmen to turn a profit found workarounds.

In 1869, a grand jury explored the prison operations, finding a nearly completed tunnel under the wall and reviewing the many rapes, thefts and other crimes committed by escaped convicts. "We are in danger of it happening again each day," the *Weekly People's Tribune* reported. "The community, rather than be exposed to these outrages, will soon take the law into their own hands."

Countless escape attempts were stopped inside the walls. But even one escaped inmate was more than the city could tolerate. In the nineteenth century, inmates walked across town to work as house servants, agricultural laborers or construction workers (including on the first Missouri Supreme Court building) and to quarry stone or macadamize streets. It was said the female inmates, too, would "wander to ply their immoral trade."

At one point, the citizens threatened to treat unguarded inmates as escapees. "Criminals locked behind prison walls might help add permanence to the new state capital, but, given access to the streets, produced a sense of peril and disorder.…It began to appear as if the town was, in fact, a prisoner of the penitentiary," Missouri historian Gary Kremer wrote in "The Prison Against the Town: Jefferson City and the Penitentiary in the 19th Century."

Too Easy for Trustees

For many of the trustees—those inmates deemed more reliable and responsible—the freedom to roam the city unguarded was too much.

Trustees Walter Brown and Leo Dupont, highway robbers from Kansas City and St. Louis, respectively, in October 1924 were sent unguarded to Prison Farm No. 3 to haul gravel. On their return to town, they found a bottle of liquor. After enjoying their "hooch," they returned to the prison, stole a car from the prison garage and found more alcohol. DuPont eventually returned to the prison, where he slept off his inebriation in the garage.

Brown, however, went to the Missouri Pacific station, where the wife of Jackson County convict J.C. Webster worked at the depot restaurant. Brown lured her, saying her husband was ill and that he had been sent for her.

After they were in the car, Brown drove toward Schubert against Mrs. Webster's protests. He put her in handcuffs and threatened her to keep quiet, holding her with one hand and driving with the other.

The car skidded on loose gravel and ran off the road into a steep embankment. A couple from Cooper County stopped after seeing the accident and took Mrs. Webster back to Jefferson City. Brown was still drunk and waiting at the car when prison officials arrived.

This event "should sound a warning bell to prison authorities that as long as convicts are permitted to roam the streets of Jefferson City at will,

The garage of the prison during Prohibition faced Lafayette Street. *Missouri State Archives, Mark Schreiber Collection.*

that no woman can leave her home with any assurance of safety," the *Daily Capital News* said.

Just a month before, three trustees—also hardened criminals with long police and prison records—took their chance in September 1924 to climb over the prison wall near the main entrance, using a ladder from the prison yard. Guards on the wall opened fire, and more pursued with sawed-off shotguns.

The escapees first huddled in a thicket near the railroad track, where it was discovered that Eddie O'Keefe had buckshot lodged in his head and neck. O'Keefe, a laundryman born in Pennsylvania, was in the first year of his five-year sentence from Jackson County for first-degree robbery.

O'Keefe and Frank Roach had been on duty as cooks in the hospital. They were joined by Black inmate Jim Swain, who was working the night shift as the messenger on duty. Roach, who had been sent to MSP by Christian County for fifteen years on a statutory offense, and Swain, doing five years from St. Joseph for second-degree burglary, continued as planned down the railroad tracks.

Then, a week later, sixty-year-old trustee J.B. Terrance simply walked away while working on the Callaway County prison farm. He had just four months remaining on his two-year sentence for grand larceny in the same county. This was his second successful escape, having eluded officers for three months the year before. His freedom was shorter the second time, as he was caught in New Bloomfield the same day.

Unreliable trustees continued to plague Jefferson City residents well into the twentieth century. A 1926 editorial in the *Jefferson City Tribune* read as follows: "It seems that the prison must have trustees and that among them are many untrustworthy trustees who every so often walk uninvited into the homes of townspeople and pick up and carry away sundry loose articles or who cop an automobile and tour the country for a week or two.…It is bad enough that the city must contend with the ex-convict without having trustees that can't be trusted running about seeking what they might purloin.…It is unfortunate indeed that the state has never had money enough to build a wall around the outlying prison buildings. Then there would be no excuse for permitting 'trustworthy' thieves to run loose."

Cole County representative David Peters introduced a bill in November 1924 that would prohibit a convict from stepping outside the prison walls unless accompanied by a guard. It included an explicit provision against prisoners driving state cars unless a guard was with them. Peters told the *Daily Capital News*: "I propose…so that it will be impossible for convicts at

Inmates regularly worked outside the confines of the Missouri State Penitentiary walls. *Missouri State Archives, Mark Schreiber Collection.*

the prison to roam the streets of Jefferson City and Cole County at all hours of the day and night....Convicts during recent years have been permitted to attend baseball games, to visit relatives in this city and to stroll unguarded around the streets. Numerous outrages have been committed by these men....The people of Cole County demand some protection and will be almost unanimously in favor of the bill....Citizens have long-protested, without avail, against the amazing and dangerous freedom and privileges allowed certain 'pets' at the prison here."

FROSTBITE TO FREEDOM

A new wall was erected across Lafayette and Water Streets in 1925. The following year, "one of the most desperate attempts ever to escape" was executed by Carl Pittman and Fred Hildebrand, according to Mark Schreiber in *Somewhere in Time*. Pittman and Hildebrand worked at the prison machine shop. One day in January 1926, while the guard's back was turned, the pair grabbed a ladder and scurried over the wall.

The Missouri River and Missouri Pacific Railroad just on the north side of the Missouri State Penitentiary wall were too enticing for many inmates to resist. *Missouri State Archives, Mark Schreiber Collection.*

They did not go unnoticed, however. Guards on Towers no. 11 and no. 12 fired at them as they ran for the frigid river. That alerted other guards, who joined in the pursuit with shotguns.

The Missouri River was not frozen over, so the would-be escapees had to jump onto ice cakes floating on the top. Hildebrand managed to make it atop one from the shore, but Pittman had to swim to another and hold on.

While struggling with the inhospitable escape method, the convicts also had bullets and cursing hurled at them from the shore. Then, when they were halfway across to the Callaway County side, the current tossed them back to the prison-side riverbank.

Exhausted and with frostbitten hands and feet, Pittman and Hildebrand took hold of the sticks offered by the guards on the bank. The convicts were wrapped in blankets and rushed to the prison hospital.

THE SEWER ROUTE

By July 1924, the popular escape routes through the sewer system or the underground steam tunnels had been barred. Many a convict prior to this intervention had crawled through the small spaces, which led out to beyond the prison walls.

Even so, Walter Hollub, an inmate from St. Louis, had been part of a work gang that dug down twenty-four inches to install a feeder sewer under the prison playground. As luck would have it, a wheelbarrow was left behind. While the guards and other criminals returned at the end of the day, Hollub was allowed unsupervised to retrieve the wheelbarrow and made his escape.

The twenty-year-old mail clerk previously had spent time in the Boonville reformatory, also for first-degree robbery. Had he stayed at the MSP, his seven-year sentence would have expired in January 1930. However, the escapee was arrested in Boulder, Colorado, and sent to the Colorado State Penitentiary, where he died in a battle with guards in October 1929.

OVER THE WALL

Of course, the icon and source of the prison's nickname, "The Walls," presented the greatest obstacle for most escapes.

A failed attempt of getting over the wall while avoiding being seen by guards or hurrying to escape them could end badly, as was the case with John Wisener in 1927. He ended up in the prison hospital with a broken leg.

Wisener, sent from St. Louis on a murder charge, and Alva Clark, serving ten years for attempting to wreck a train in Buchanan County, left a prison factory intending to climb the wall at the former female department. They put on civilian clothes, pretended to be wall repairmen and made it to the other side with the ruse. Wisener stole a parked car on Water Street but was recaptured near the broom factory at Marshall and Water Streets.

Clark had strapped a long knife to his waist and used it to threaten employee Robert Mueller, who was getting ready to leave. Mueller managed to hold his car door shut while he started the car and put it in drive. This caused Clark to fall from the running board. Mueller then entered the prison to sound the alarm as Clark ran west on Water Street. He was soon recaptured.

Walking Away

The easiest escapes for convicts were made while they were on work crews outside the prison. The prison had farms and quarries that were worked in uncontained environments. Inmates also were used for other labor projects, such as improving the Capitol grounds.

That's how J.A. Gibbs escaped in November 1924. He was part of a work gang raking leaves and conducting other projects for statehouse landscaping. Guards thought he may have hidden in the Capitol's large basement or at Miss Eugene Dennis's hotel. But Dennis told them the escapee, a chauffeur serving a three-year sentence for larceny from Cape Girardeau, headed to St. Louis by way of the railroad. Three weeks later, he was returned to the MSP from Cape Girardeau County.

TB Ward Hero

An unknown number of attempted escapes never posed a threat to residents of Jefferson City because they were stopped within the walls.

The old hospital at the Missouri State Penitentiary. *Missouri State Archives, Mark Schreiber Collection.*

In October 1926, trustee Ollie Cooper not only saved the life of Captain C.L. Fleeman but also slowed the escape of seven inmates armed with knives and guns.

A forty-seven-year-old patient in the tuberculosis ward of the prison hospital, Cooper saw the would-be escapees enter and stab Fleeman. Cooper knocked down one attacker, blocking a doorway, and drove back the others with the butt of a revolver he had wrested from another.

The inmates had smashed in a window at B Hall, where they disarmed Captain T.J. Wines before they made their break. After being deterred by Cooper in the hospital, the seven men barricaded themselves inside the shirt factory, where they held off guards for two hours. Eventually, a band of guards used the rear entrance to gain the advantage. After a "barrage of gunshots," the convicts surrendered, according to Mark Schreiber in *Somewhere in Time.*

The next day, Governor Sam Baker invited Cooper and three other prisoners who helped prevent this escape to see him at his office, where he granted all of them unconditional paroles.

Cooper, who grew up in Maryland, had come to the prison from Butler County with a three-year sentence for burglary after serving a term for theft at the Arkansas state prison.

Unfortunately, Cooper returned to the prison only four months after his unexpected parole. And four months after that, he was dead. Within a few days of arriving back in Poplar Bluff, he was caught burglarizing a store. He and another inmate in the Poplar Bluff jail made a "sensational jailbreak," but he was found in Little Rock, Arkansas, visiting his wife.

Cooper was returned to the MSP tuberculosis ward, where he was killed by inmate Reuben Bobbits on June 14, 1927, with a knife to the heart. Speculation was that inmates did not like how Cooper had "snitched" on the attempted escapees at their subsequent trial. Lifer Bobbits, thirty-three, claimed that the fight was over a card game after Cooper threw a chair at him.

Cooper, who was a private with the Arkansas Army Service Corps, is buried at Jefferson City National Cemetery.

MUTINY

THE OTHER RIOT AT THE MSP

About 750 men sat down for the noon meal in the prison dining hall, as they did every day. But on this day in March 1930, they did not get up afterward and go back to their work in the factories or other duties. In a nonviolent act, as a group, they sat in protest of the poor food, overcrowding and long hours they were subjected to at the prison's factories.

Deputy Warden W.D. Long first tried encouraging the men to go back to their afternoon locations. When that didn't work, the men beat on the tables and cried for "meat." The iron gate at Lafayette Street to the office entrance was locked, and a "big Negro convict" was placed outside the gate to turn back visitors and media.

By 1:50 p.m. on March 26, the governor had been informed and declared a state of emergency in Cole County.

Warden Leslie Rudolph ironically was at the prison farm seven miles east, conferring with architects for the proposed $750,000 intermediate reformatory, which would alleviate one of the inmates' main concerns: overcrowding. Governor Henry Caulfield, who stayed up-to-date on the situation by telephone, also happened to be holding a hearing on the future first-time-offender prison in the Capitol House lounge.

On his return, Warden Rudolph entered the dining room alone to talk down the protest. "We want you to have plenty to eat and we want it to be good food," the warden told them.

Eight prison guards were outside with guns and tear bombs. And the local Missouri National Guard unit was on its way, following Caulfield's

On the first day of the 1930 mutiny, media and citizens were blocked from access and information to what was happening inside the walls. *Missouri State Archives, Mark Schreiber Collection.*

executive order, which approved the "use of such military forces of state necessary for preservation of life and property and the maintenance of law and order."

The local unit was the headquarters company for the 70th Infantry Brigade, commanded by a Captain Holliway and assisted by Lieutenant Lee Yaple. Twenty-one soldiers and thirteen members of the 128th Field Artillery Band were armed and ready for duty at the penitentiary within forty minutes.

The three dozen guardsmen arrived just as the inmates were filing out of the dining hall in an orderly fashion, having given Warden Rudolph a round of applause for his speech of understanding and willingness to explore their complaints.

The prison population topped out at 4,060 in a facility designed for a maximum of 2,600. Although plans already were underway for what became Algoa Correctional Center, it was early in the discussion, and this event helped lend a sense of urgency.

In addition to overcrowding, the inmates also had a legitimate complaint of poor food. That day, they had raw potatoes in their Irish stew, the result of faulty boilers. The stew recipe included 1,600 pounds of fresh beef without the bone, four barrels of potatoes, seventy-five gallons of tomatoes and seven bushels of onions. The remainder of the menu was chowchow, creamed potatoes, green beans, bread and coffee.

And inmates wanted more meat, which the officials had cut back on as a cost-saving measure while feeding so many inmates. At the time, at least two meals each week included roast beef, pork roast, beef heart or spare ribs.

The dining hall was the source of the inmates' frustration during the 1930 mutiny as well as the location for the largest protests. *Missouri State Archives, Mark Schreiber Collection.*

For their evening meal, the menu was stewed prunes, bread, syrup and coffee. The rest of the evening went according to routine at the prison. But a plot emerged that included a workers' strike, burning at least two factories and rioting.

Rudolph's investigation validated the inmates' complaints.

The next morning, hundreds of breakfasting inmates again refused to leave the dining room while their counterparts were already at work in the prison factories. The protesters began by banging on the tables, and things escalated to throwing plates and cutlery, breaking windows and turning over food supplies in the kitchen.

Inmates in other parts of the prison could hear the din, which signaled other prisoners to make their move. At the chair factory, fifty men refused to work, and the strike spread to the overalls, broom, shirt, pants and twine factories. At that point, the protesting workers were taken to their cells. Only the chair factory, where one hundred men were not involved in the strike, remained functioning.

Governor Caulfield personally visited the prison early on the second day to talk with the prison board, and the local National Guard unit was called back, remaining until 2:00 p.m.

At 11:00 a.m. on the second day, the 138th Infantry from St. Louis mobilized as a provisional machine-gun company and arrived in Jefferson City at 5:00 p.m. with two officers and twenty-eight enlisted men. One machine gun was placed on the second floor of the warden's office, and the other one was positioned opposite the dining hall across the courtyard. These soldiers remained on active duty for another five days until noon on April 2.

Unlike the previous day, media, citizen-volunteers and officials were allowed into the prison. Police Chief Harry Parker said his entire force was available to the prison. Police and local citizen-volunteers were armed with handguns and shotguns, waiting in the warden's office as a reserve force. The fire department sent most of its manpower in case the fire threat became a reality. A traffic officer at the intersection of Lafayette Street and Capitol Avenue helped limit traffic in front of the prison.

The St. Louis Police Department provided tear-gas bombs, which were delivered within an hour from Lambert Field to the Jefferson Airfield, about where Turkey Creek Golf Center is today, by the Thirty-Fifth Division Aviation.

Wearing a long coat and a broad-brimmed hat, Warden Rudolph was at the front of about fifty guards when the tear gas was thrown into the dining hall. About 350 inmates who had been trapped in the dining hall with the miscreants quickly exited the building and complied with guards. The others continued to be contrary, receiving blows from the guards' clubs. But no shots were fired.

When things were at their most heated, even the prison clerk, W.B. Hodge, could not remain behind his desk in the administration building. He grabbed a club alongside the guards at the dining hall, and when dishes were thrown out the window, he threw them right back in.

About 1,200 inmates were counted among the uprising; only 165 prison guards were on duty. An estimated 400 prisoners were deemed rebellious. The other 800 were thought to have followed out of fear for their own safety. By the afternoon of the second day, about 80 percent of the 4,000 total convicts had been locked in their cells. Prison officials acknowledged that many inmates were not part of the mutiny, but it was precautionary following the closing of the factories.

Guards began identifying potential ringleaders, who were separated and placed in solitary confinement in I Hall. Confinement was one of the lighter

The Housing Unit I Hall was designed for the hardest of the convicts. Ringleaders of the 1930 mutiny were held in confinement here. *Missouri State Archives, Mark Schreiber Collection.*

forms of punishment. For example, most inmates were being released by the three-quarters rule, meaning that, on good behavior, they served out only 75 percent of the length of their original sentence. But the ringleaders were promised that they would remain for the entire sentence. "We have treated them well, but they have shown no appreciation," prison board chairman Frank B. Jones said in the *Jefferson City Post-Tribune*. "Now the most stringent penal regulations will be enforced."

Other new regulations were introduced to change the prison approach from "Sunday school to real prison." Radios were taken from cells, playground privileges were revoked and the silent system was renewed in the dining hall. Those identified as the ringleaders were not only placed in solitary confinement but also were issued the iconic black-and-white-striped uniforms, which had been discarded years before.

Warden Rudolph told the media: "I've tried to treat these men right. The food has been good and despite the extremely crowded conditions, we have endeavored to use kindness, instead of force. But the men failed to appreciate it and from now on this prison will be ruled by force, instead of kindness. The coddling of convicts has stopped, let the reformers say what they will. We are forced now to resort to some of the older penal methods, to avoid chaotic conditions here."

Once things settled down, on the third day, the warden met with more than one hundred of the suspected instigators, who had been placed in solitary confinement. One by one, an inmate was brought out to the courtyard, where the guards informed the warden of his reputation and disposition. More than sixty were sent back to their former cells; forty were retained in solitary. Most of the suspected ringleaders were white, from St. Louis or Kansas City and in prison for theft.

"We do not know what to expect next, but we will keep in readiness to meet any emergency," the warden told the *Post-Tribune*.

The noon meal on the third day was served with the prison band playing, as was typical. But outside the dining hall, the two National Guard machine guns, which could fire six hundred bullets in one minute, were still fixed on the building.

The ringleaders had been narrowed down to twenty-two, and seven were placed in solitary indefinitely.

The prison hospital treated sixty-two convicts for injuries in those three days, not all inflicted by the guards. Eight men sustained injuries requiring them to remain at the hospital, including Tony Noto, a St. Louis bigamist, who had a broken skull.

The penitentiary was noticeably quiet on the third night.

By March 30, privileges were returned to those not involved in the mutiny. Factory work resumed gradually, with estimates of the prison losing $25,000 for the days the factories were not in operation. By April 1, three factories were at full capacity. The twine, broom and shoe factories were not in operation, but prison officials said that decision had more to do with an overstock of inventory.

The prison population, minus the instigators confined at I Hall, returned to normal routines for the most part under the watch of the National Guard machine guns.

The governor praised the prison authorities, who "admirably handled" the situation, without shots fired or loss of life.

19

WILLIAM BULLARD

FIRST MISSOURI CORRECTIONS OFFICER
TO DIE IN THE LINE OF DUTY

The first corrections officer in Missouri to lose his life in the line of duty was also the victim of the second known murder in Jefferson City.

A plot to kill William Bullard, take his weapons and keys and escape through the front gate had been developing for weeks. In June 1841, Bullard was turnkey and general superintendent within the five-year-old Missouri State Penitentiary.

Prior to Bullard's death, inmate Henry Cortmier, twenty-one, was shot by overseer Henry Lane in August 1839. Born in Germany, Cortmier was serving three years for grand larceny from St. Louis. Lane was publicly executed for the crime two months later.

On this fateful day, Bullard was left in charge of the convicts left behind, while overseer John Gordon took about twenty inmates to High Street on a building project. The other overseer, Nelson Burch, was away on business. That left Bullard inside the wall with one sentinel in the watchtower.

Inmates William Rogers, William H. Berry and J.B. Richards worked on the second floor of the saddlery. After lunch, the three men asked Bullard to the shop to give them instructions for their work. While Richards asked him a question, Rogers struck Bullard in the head with a mallet. Then Berry sprang upon Bullard and held him down while Rogers bludgeoned him. Bullard died about two hours after the attack.

Bullard was born in Tennessee, and his family moved to Missouri, where he was orphaned in Boone County. He and his wife, Rebecca (Housten), had recently welcomed their first infant son, Reuben. His marker at the Woodland–Old City Cemetery is worn and faded.

"The most daring deed of murder was committed in the penitentiary in this city," the *Jefferson Inquirer* reported.

The inmate trio took Bullard's keys and two pistols. Six other inmates followed them through the front gate. "The alarm and bustle, brought nearly all the convicts to the gate, when some who were opposed to the desperate undertaking, shut the gate and placing themselves in an attitude of defense, prevented the escape of the others until the arrival of a young man employed as a mechanic," the newspaper said.

French-born Richards, twenty-two, was sick and unable to keep up. He was caught the same day. A harness maker sent from St. Louis on a three-year sentence for grand larceny, Richards died of disease a year after the escape attempt.

Rogers, Berry and the other six headed to the Missouri River and hid in deep ravines and dense woods, evading the community mob searching for them. The escapees' tracks were covered by new crime. They entered the home of a Mr. Locke on the Osage River. They plundered the old man's house, took his last bit of clothing and everything else. Then they crossed the Osage River heading south.

The state offered a reward of $500 for their capture, and the lessees of the prison added $400.

James Fugate, fifty-five, a Virginia-born house carpenter, was returned five days after the escape. He also was serving a three-year sentence from St. Louis for grand larceny. William Meyers, twenty-eight, was returned a week afterward. The Kentucky-born counterfeiter escaped again in October 1841 but was captured the same day.

Berry, an eighteen-year-old saddler born in Kentucky, was returned on June 27, 1841. He was three months into a two-year sentence for grand larceny from Clinton County. He was the only one hanged for the murder of Bullard, on February 10, 1842.

Thomas Finn, thirty, and John Callahan, twenty-six, returned the same day as Berry. Finn, an English sailor, was three years into a ten-year sentence from St. Louis for murder, for which he was later pardoned. Callahan, a miller born in New York, was serving seven years from St. Louis for counterfeiting.

The last of the escapees to be returned were blacksmith William Johnson and cotton farmer M. Boden. They were caught crossing the Mississippi River above Alton, Illinois. Johnson, twenty-eight, escaped and was returned twice more before being pardoned for second-degree murder and grand larceny from Jefferson County. Boden successfully escaped again in February 1842, evading a ten-year sentence for robbery from St. Louis.

Only the ringleader, William Rogers, never returned. An eighteen-year-old saddler born in New Jersey, Rogers had been sent from Jefferson County in March of that year on a forty-four-year sentence for robbery and horse stealing. He was believed to have drowned in the crossing with Johnson and Boden.

A problem that plagued the prison for nearly a century was poor conditions. This, combined with easy opportunities, provoked inmates to continue escape attempts.

A committee toured the prison in 1842, reporting to the Missouri General Assembly. They found the prisoners were badly clothed, dirty and in miserable condition, having scarce bedding, suffering from cold with no fire and receiving little food. Instead of a hospital, lessees would take sick prisoners to their own homes. The number of inmates had increased already from 44 to 150 in four years. One small cell held up to 10 convicts.

Governor Thomas Reynolds made a plea that was repeated and ignored for decades: "I would respectfully urge the propriety of confining the convicts to labor within the walls of the prison. A contrary policy is at war with the nature and design of the penitentiary system."

20

ELI JENKINS

UNNECESSARY VIOLENCE

A beloved teacher at the Missouri State Penitentiary, Eli Whitney Jenkins grew up in Loose Creek and worked farms in Greenfield and in Kansas before teaching in Sedalia. He moved to Jefferson City about 1907, when he began working at the Missouri State Penitentiary.

His sixty-seven-year life ended on February 28, 1918, when three inmates under the age of twenty-five, attempting to escape the prison, stabbed the wall guard to death. Jenkins was "one of the kindest prison guards....The first man to start educational work at the Missouri State Penitentiary among the convicts, devoting extra hours of his time each evening to instructing a group of prisoners," the *St. Louis Globe Democrat* reported.

Jenkins was responsible for waking up the cooks in B Hall, the newest of the cell houses, so they could begin breakfast at 4:30 a.m. On the fateful day, David Bartlett pretended to be sick in his cell. Kenneth Brewer and an inmate named Goss contributed to the lie when Jenkins came to wake them for their work detail.

When Jenkins entered the cell to check on Bartlett, Bartlett struck the elderly guard twice over the head with a two-foot-long lead pipe. When that did not knock Jenkins down, Jenkins tried to draw his pistol. That's when Bartlett pulled out a large butcher knife and stabbed him three times near the heart.

Later, Bartlett said he only meant to stun Jenkins. "I was badly excited," the inmate told the prison board in his confession.

Brewer took Jenkins's shoes and then used the keys to free Joe Kenney from a nearby cell. Bartlett took the guard's coat and pistol. Then they left Goss bound and gagged on his bunk.

Bartlett, Brewer and Kenney ran to the east stockade wall, where they used boards to climb over the first wall and then a ladder to climb down from the guardhouse. They ran across the playgrounds to the outer wall, where they used the boards again to climb up and then jumped to the ground. The trio boarded a baggage car of the Missouri Pacific's fast mail train at Jefferson City.

They arrived at 5:00 a.m. in Sedalia, hiding in a shanty near the railroad tracks. Police discovered them still wearing their prison uniforms later that day when the convicts approached the train station looking for a freight train headed west.

On their return to the MSP, the trio were placed in special receiving cells away from the regular population, "for fear that angry mobs of convicts might do them harm," Mark Schreiber wrote in *Somewhere in Time.* "The other prisoners were deeply ashamed of the actions of their 'brothers' and threatened to string up the three, if they ever caught sight of them at large in the prison proper."

Bartlett, whose nickname was "Cockey," was charged with the murder in March 1918, while Brewer and Kenney were charged as accessories.

The *Post-Tribune* described Bartlett as "a little, undersized fellow…[with] the look of a degenerate." He had been sentenced in 1915 by Cooper County to six years for felonious assault. Another ninety-nine years were added for second-degree murder.

Bartlett made two more escape attempts in 1923. In the spring, he sawed out of a cell building and scaled the wall but was soon returned. In the fall, while working the prison's rock pile, he attempted to reach freedom through the prison sewer. Several inmates had had success with the route, but iron bars had been installed recently. Bartlett and another lifer, Thomas Seminary, were found standing neck-deep in ice water and nearly frozen to death.

A blacksmith born in Alabama, Kenney also made further escape attempts. In September 1921, he was part of a group led by Dan Hogan that planned to seize a switch engine when it backed a car of coal next to the powerhouse. Hogan, who was serving ten years for robbery, wrapped a large iron hammer with an old cloth and hid it in his coat. He knocked out prison guard James Tise, who was near the powerhouse, and took his pistol. When foreman Leeland Gordon tried to help Tise, Hogan struck him, too. Armed with two pistols and a derringer, Hogan forced foreman Frank Young to the powerhouse.

While climbing into the engine's cab, Hogan was shot by guard Dexter Rowland. The convict fell, breaking his leg. Rowland then shot Kenney three times as he attempted to climb into the coal car. Only in his first of twenty-three years working at the prison, Rowland later served nine years on the Jefferson City Police force.

Sam Taylor, who had a life sentence for first-degree murder, and Dick Kennedy, in for highway robbery, were too weak to make the run, which likely saved their lives from a total of nearly thirty shots fired by prison guards.

21

HENRY SPIEKER

YOUNG FARMER GUNNED DOWN BY ESCAPEE

A young local farmer lost his life on May 9, 1899, during a manhunt for escaped prisoner Joshua L. Craft. A train robber, Craft had fled his home of Texas, where he had robbed a train, when he was caught in Lawrence County for doing the same thing, earning a fifteen-year sentence.

Three years in, Craft and fellow inmate Ed Krash escaped. Wearing citizens' clothing, the pair stole a delivery wagon and fled south at high speed through the city streets. At Swifts Highway, the horse and buggy overturned, and the two men ran on foot. Krash made a successful escape from Jefferson City, then was killed in a train wreck at Springfield.

Craft stole a loaded Winchester rifle and a horse from John Heidker, a farmer living with his older sister Catha, on their family farm. Local farmers joined prison guards in tracking Craft. The first to happen on to the escapee was young Henry Spieker. Only twenty-two, Spieker told the criminal to surrender. That's when Craft fatally shot Spieker in the abdomen.

Craft again took off running, but he was soon overtaken by Deputy Constable James Crump. Craft attempted to shoot Crump, but his weapon jammed. Crump then shot the convict in the head, causing only a scalp wound, and then returned him to the prison, where Craft was placed in solitary confinement.

Sentenced to hang for first-degree murder, Craft received a stay of execution from Governor Alexander Dockery after his fellow convicts raised sixty-five dollars to help pay for his mother to travel from Texas to see him before his death. Despite an anonymous assassination threat, the governor dismissed a petition for commutation.

Craft was hanged at the Cole County Jail at 9:02 a.m. on January 21, 1902. Unlike the previous six executions, it was not a clean death. The rope, which had not been waxed, slipped, causing the noose to be out of proper position behind Craft's ear. Craft struggled and pled for someone to end it before he died, not of a broken neck but of strangulation.

SOUTH SIDE WAGON CHASE

TRIPLE HANGING FOLLOWED SPECTACULAR ESCAPE

Hidden underneath a workbench in the leather room of the prison shoe factory were four Colt .44 revolvers, more than one hundred rounds of ammunition and nitroglycerin. Just two weeks after being released from the prison, H.E. Spencer had climbed into the prison to deposit the items to aid the escape attempt of George Ryan, Harry Vaughan, Edward Raymond, Hiram Black and Eli Ziegler.

All of the men worked in the prison shoe shop and there made their pact and plan. On the day of his release, the other inmates gave Spencer forty dollars for the supplies. The pistols were bought from a Kansas City pawn shop, and the nitroglycerin, fuses and caps were taken from mining camps in the Joplin-Carthage area.

At 3:00 p.m. on November 24, 1905, while working in the shoe factory, the convicts armed themselves. The plan was to take advantage of the absence of Warden Matt Hall and six other prison guards, who were transferring seventy-one federal prisoners to Fort Leavenworth, Kansas, that day.

The first step was entering Deputy Warden R.E. See's office, which was on the ground floor and opened out into the yard. They ordered him to put up his hands. Instead, the veteran law enforcement officer reached for his weapon. Black fired, wounding the warden in the wrist as well as his accomplice Vaughan, who was reaching for See's weapon at the same time.

Jacob Wegman and Theodore Perting, both of Loose Creek, had the unfortunate position to be visitors sitting in See's office at the time. The visitors and the deputy warden were taken as human shields as the escapees ran across the yard to the wagon entrance.

About that same time, gatekeeper John Clay had opened the inner gate for Charles Woodland, who was driving a two-horse wagon of supplies for the shoe shops. The convicts and their hostages rushed through the inner gate and shouted at Clay to show his hands. As Clay was raising his hands higher, Vaughan shot him in the neck, killing him instantly.

The discharge of gunpowder in the enclosed space burned Deputy Warden See's face, yet the escaping inmates demanded he unlock the outside doors. He told them he did not know how, suggesting they go through the office. That's when guard Ephraim Allison appeared at the grated door to see what was happening. Shots were exchanged, and Allison was fatally shot twice. One of the convicts at this point shouted, "Kill them all, let's shoot our way out."

See was shot in the shoulder and fell to the ground, while Perting and Wegman ran free of their convict-captors. Guard J.K. Young responded from the upstairs armory. After seeing Allison's body on the floor, Young approached the door to the wagon entrance and was shot. Guard John Bruner also ran toward the sound. As he looked through a small hole in the door, one of the convicts shot at him.

The inmates put the nitroglycerin to use, blowing a three-and-a-half-foot hole in the forty-by-fifteen-foot double steel outer gate. Four of them, minus Zeigler, emerged onto Lafayette Street, where another guard saw them shouting and armed. He dropped his shotgun and fell to the ground, pretending to be hit.

Once free from the prison walls, the four escapees ran west down State Street toward the Missouri Pacific depot. They were immediately pursued by See, who, despite having wounds in his wrist and shoulder, had grabbed the weapon dropped by the outside guard.

Bruner joined the pursuit on foot, as did J.K. Young, who was shot in the thigh as shots were exchanged. "Pedestrians jumped behind trees and obstacles to avoid bullets," a newspaper reported.

An expert marksman, Bruner was able to shoot twenty-one-year-old Black before the four reached the Missouri Pacific depot. Wisconsin-born Black had been sentenced to three years for burglary from Grundy County as a member of the Spickard gang. He died from his wounds not long after.

The plan to steal a locomotive centered on Black, who had experience driving trains. That left the remaining three to improvise. Teamster Arthur Lane had the unfortunate circumstance of sitting on a wagon at the depot,

The deadliest escape attempt in the history of the Missouri State Penitentiary took the life of two guards before the four convicts blew a hole in the outside gate with nitroglycerin. *Missouri State Archives, Mark Schreiber Collection.*

waiting to pick up the next run of luggage and other transfer items for the Houck McHenry Express Company. The three escapees jumped into Lane's wagon, throwing him to the floor.

They drove the horses at a high speed west on Water Street to the Governor's Mansion, then south on Madison Street through the business district. Asked for directions out of the city, Lane led them on a circuitous route around the South Side, giving the pursuing prison guards time to catch up.

In the pursuit wagon from the prison, guard J.G. Williams of Morgan County and Young gave chase through the city streets. "The whole city was thrilled with terror and amazement," the *Nevada Weekly Post* reported. More officers and armed citizens joined the chase.

While bullets were being exchanged, Russellville-born Lane was helpless on the wagon floor, barely escaping harm from bullets splintering the wagon. He would retell his story for decades of how bullets tore through his clothing.

"We saw them driving south for some distance, the horses galloping and running at great speed, followed by citizens afoot, and by horse and buggy, exchanging gunfire, Western movie–style, real and much alive," said Louis Haas, who stood in front of his workplace at the Capitol City Brewery.

Outside the Capitol City Brewery, in the 100 block of West Dunklin Street, Ryan fell from the wagon, firing his weapon at brewery president Andrew Jacob Moerschel, who took charge of him until prison officials picked him up.

Vaughan and Raymond attempted to continue down Dunklin Street until another brewery employee, Leonard Green, twenty-four, "bravely ran into the street, grabbed the bridle of one of the horses and stopped the wagon." Enraged, Vaughan shouted at the youth to let go. When he didn't, the inmate jumped off the wagon, ran toward the boy and pulled the hammer back on his weapon. Thankfully, when Vaughan pulled the trigger, nothing happened. The surprise created the opening for Green to wrest the weapon away from Vaughan.

At the same time, Policeman George Staihr, who had joined the chase at High Street in a light buggy, arrived. With the help of wagon owner Houck McHenry, George Walthers and Gerhart Crevelt, they held the two convicts at gunpoint until others arrived.

"It is right laughable to think how that affair turned out, so very different from our plans. When we thought we were driving out of town, we were simply going around in a circle," Raymond said.

This was not Vaughan's first deadly exchange with law enforcement. He had been sentenced to MSP from St. Louis following a shoot-out of police and the Morrison-Rosenau gang. Three detectives and two gang members died in that exchange. Vaughan survived by chance, having left the hideout just minutes before the observing cops made their fatal entry.

Warden See, who was engaged in the entire pursuit, refused to have his wounds treated until the three fugitives had been returned to the prison, where they remained in solitary confinement for nineteen months until their execution.

Bruner, fifty, said, "See is the gamest man I ever saw." And State Treasurer Jacob Gmelich, who witnessed the chase, agreed: "I have never seen anything to equal the bravery of that man."

Bruner later served four terms as Jefferson Township constable and was "known for his fearlessness and ability to hunt down criminals," including the murderer of restaurant owner Robert Tritsch, the *Jefferson City Post-Tribune* said. Before his thirty-four years as a prison guard, Bruner had been deputy sheriff in Carroll County.

Governor Joseph Folk offered a $300 reward for the arrest of accomplice Spencer, who was never found.

Deputy Warden See had served as Warren County sheriff and Missouri Supreme Court marshal before being appointed to the Missouri State Penitentiary. *Missouri State Archives, Mark Schreiber Collection.*

The community was left to recuperate from such an audacious and violent event, which took the lives of two of their neighbors, wounded others and threatened everyone. Inside the prison, Gatling guns were ordered. Outside the walls, two funerals followed.

John Albert Clay was forty-seven and left widow Mary Agnes with three children, ages fifteen, eleven and ten. His funeral at Woodland–Old City Cemetery, where Governor Folk spoke, drew three thousand mourners. Born in Virginia, he had been a farmer in Callaway County and a streetcar conductor in St. Louis before being appointed as prison guard. One newspaper described Clay as "a man of fine physique and splendid citizenship." His brother Charles was a city alderman at the time.

Ephraim Ball Allison, seventy, was buried in his hometown of Clinton, with Warden Hall giving the eulogy. Allison was remembered for "nobility of mind and kindly Christian spirit," the *Henry County Democrat* reported. A Confederate captain during the Civil War, he survived service with the Sixteenth Missouri Infantry Regiment, which saw more death than any other Missouri Confederate regiment. Allison had been a merchant and served as Henry County treasurer and presiding judge before his appointment as a "cop of the yard" at the prison.

Governor Folk proposed that the Missouri General Assembly erect monuments for both Clay and Allison inscribed with "He died at the post of duty." Although that did not materialize, the legislature did approve $2,500 to each widow.

Future mayor and state representative Edwin Silver, whose law office was at 204 East High Street, provided the murderers' defense.

The first trial resulted in a hung jury, blamed on the "overzealous methods" to prevent an escape by the trio. Prison guards stood behind each of the convicts in the courtroom with weapons ready throughout the trial. The courtroom was packed in March 1906 to hear the ruling that all three were found guilty of first-degree murder. But that decision also was interrupted, as the Missouri Supreme Court ruled that the judge's instructions to the jury should not have said the sentence should be for all three or none of them.

Finally, in January 1907, the Cole County Circuit Court gave separate verdicts and sentenced all three to execution. This time, the Missouri Supreme Court agreed with the lower court, and the governor ignored appeals for clemency.

In the spring between the decision and the execution, Deputy Warden See, fifty-six, died as a result of his wounds. The 1909 Missouri General Assembly approved a $2,000 relief bill for his widow, Laura. Before taking the deputy warden position, See had served six years as the marshal of the Missouri Supreme Court. Before that, See served two terms as Montgomery County sheriff.

A huge crowd gathered in front of the Monroe Street jail yard on the morning of June 27, 1907. Women were standing on balconies overlooking the gallows, and crowds filled local homes and "High School Hill."

Guard Howard Manchester had the death watch. Then, at 5:00 a.m., a small black wagonette arrived at the same prison entrance where the condemned had taken the lives of the two guards two years earlier. Two men with Winchester rifles stepped out of the wagon and walked alongside it as it passed through the iron gates into the prison yard.

The wagon pulled up to the oldest cellhouse, A Hall, where more guards with Winchesters escorted the three men, who were closely shackled together.

Three prison guards—Charles Kaufman, Buck Williams and W.D. Morris—entered the wagon with the three inmates. The new deputy warden, Porter Gilvin, and the yardmaster, Emmet Page, followed in a second wagon.

Although it was early morning, crowds had lined the city streets to view the procession to the Cole County Jail, where at 9:30 a.m. the inmates' death warrants were read and they were given the last sacrament by Reverend Henry Geisert. None of the three gave a statement.

The scaffold had been built to hide as much public view as possible, allowing only about two hundred of the five hundred ticket applicants inside. Among the witnesses were the widows of Clay and Allison.

Sheriff John W. Scott sprang the trap set for three. He was assisted by Howard County sheriff George Gibson, who put the noose around Raymond's neck, making it Gibson's eleventh hanging. Boone County sheriff Fountain Rothwell prepared Ryan, and Adair County sheriff John Curry was stationed with Vaughan.

Geisert claimed the bodies as a friend, had caskets waiting and saw them interred at the state graveyard at the southeast corner of Dunklin

Right: Most of the known hangings in Jefferson City took place in the lot south of the old Cole County Jail on Monroe Street. *Library of Congress*.

Below: The only triple hanging in Jefferson City history was held behind the Cole County Jail and drew hundreds, who caught a glimpse over the high fence. *Missouri State Archives, Mark Schreiber Collection*.

and Chestnut Streets, where the Lincoln University Inman Page Library fountain is today.

Raymond was a Massachusetts-born tailor, and a rumor circulated that the twenty-six-year-old had graduated from Harvard University. He arrived at the prison in December 1904 for a five-year sentence from St. Louis City for first-degree robbery after he held up a saloon and five customers.

Also a saloon robber, Ryan, twenty-seven, was called the "icebox robber" after putting the bartender and two patrons into the saloon icebox before taking seventeen dollars from the cash register. He had arrived for his second stay at the prison, having also served eighteen months at Leavenworth, Kansas, in March 1904 on an eight-year sentence for first-degree robbery from Jackson County.

Vaughan, alias H.B. Adams, the most hardened of the three, had been sentenced three times to the MSP, as well as two years at the Ohio State Penitentiary. His first term began in 1891, when he was eighteen, for burglary from St. Louis County. A year after he was discharged, he returned in 1896 for shooting a brakeman and for train robbery in 1895 from Vernon County. Fellow train robbers William Rogers and William Morris also were sentenced to the MSP, where the former died by eating soap. After their release in June 1904, Vaughan and Morris soon joined the St. Louis gang. Morris was killed in the shootout, and Vaughan returned to the MSP in April 1905, seven months before the escape attempt.

Had Vaughn made good his escape, the Ohio-born shoemaker would have been made the leader of a new gang of burglars and safeblowers in Kansas and Missouri. That is what Spencer, who was released from a two-year sentence from Bates County for possession of burglary tools, was supposed to have been organizing. Spencer was never found.

BIBLIOGRAPHY

Chapter 1

Boone's Lick Times (Fayette, MO), February 19, 1842; May 28, 1842.

Brooks, Michelle. "The Hanging of Dedimus Buell Burr in 1842." Historic City of Jefferson Cole County History series. *Jefferson City (MO) News Tribune*, 2021.

Bryan, William, and Robert Rose. *A History of the Pioneer Families of Missouri*. St. Louis, MO: Bryan Brand & Company, 1876.

Cole County Circuit Court. Cole County, Missouri.

Cole County Recorder of Deeds marriage records. Cole County, Missouri.

Haddam County, Connecticut, Court of Probate. May 20, 1833.

James Ford. *History of Jefferson City*. Jefferson City, MO: New Day Press, 1935.

Jefferson Enquirer (Jefferson City, MO), 1842.

Schreiber, Mark. *Somewhere in Time: 170 Years of Missouri Corrections*. Jefferson City, MO: Missouri Department of Corrections, 1991.

State Journal (Jefferson City, MO), April 24, 1874.

Sunday News and Tribune (Jefferson City, MO), May 24, 1936.

U.S. Census.

Wiscombe, Erold Clark. "The Descendants of Maria Burr, John W. Clark and William West Lane." N.p.: self-published, 1975.

Chapter 2

Annual Report of the Adjutant General of Missouri. Jefferson City, MO: W.A. Curry, 1864.

Blevins, Robin. *Cole County Sheriff's Office and Jail History*. Jefferson City, MO: Cole County Sheriff's Department, n.d.

Cole County Recorder of Deeds. Cole County, Missouri.

Goldammer, Deborah. Unpublished notes "Outlot 6." Jefferson City, Missouri.

Missouri Volksfreund (Jefferson City, MO), translated Walter Schroeder, October 18, 1876; October 20, 1876; December 20, 1876.

People's Tribune (Jefferson City, MO), July 25, 1866.

Reverend Haas. Journal. Central United Church of Christ archives. Jefferson City, Missouri.

Schroeder, Walter. Unpublished letter to author, 2022.

State Journal (Jefferson City, MO), May 30, 1873; October 22, 1875; May 19, 1876; October 20, 1876; October 27, 1876; August 10, 1877; December 14, 1877.

U.S. Census.

Chapter 3

Ancestry. World War II Draft Cards. Young Men, 1940–47. www.ancestry.com.

Daily Capital News (Jefferson City, MO), May 25, 1934.

Jefferson City (MO) Cole County Democrat, October 2, 1890.

Jefferson City (MO) News and Tribune, January 21, 1934; April 7, 1934; April 8, 1934; May 27, 1934; June 3, 1934; December 30, 1934.

Jefferson City (MO) Post-Tribune, February 27, 1934; April 2, 1934; April 3, 1934; April 4, 1934; April 5, 1934; April 10, 1934; April 13, 1934; April 26, 1934; May 23, 1934; May 24, 1934; May 25, 1934; October 28, 1940; March 3, 1941.

Jefferson City (MO) State Republican, October 2, 1890.

Jefferson City Police Department. Plaque.

Kansas City (MO) Times, September 26, 1890.

Missouri Death Certificate. Missouri State Archives. Jefferson City, Missouri. https://s1.sos.mo.gov/records/Archives/ArchivesMvc/DeathCertificates.

Rolla (MO) Herald, January 8, 1891.

U.S. Census

Chapter 4

Clarion (Lincoln University, MO), February 5, 1943.

Cole County Probate. Wills. Vol. D.

Jefferson City city directory. Missouri State Archives. 1904; 1921. https:// www.sos.mo.gov/mdh/CityDirectories.

Jefferson City (MO) Tribune, May 10, 1926; May 11, 1926; May 12, 1926; May 14, 1926; May 18, 1926; May 21, 1926; May 22, 1926; June 14, 1926; June 16, 1926; June 18, 1926; June 22, 1926; June 28, 1926; June 30, 1926; July 9, 1926; September 20, 1926; October 19, 1926; October 20, 1926; November 5, 1926; December 7, 1926.

Missouri State Penitentiary Database. Missouri State Archives. Jefferson City, Missouri. https://s1.sos.mo.gov/records/archives/archivesdb/msp.

U.S. Census.

Chapter 5

Brooks, Michelle. *Lost Jefferson City*. Charleston, SC: The History Press, 2022.

Daily Capital News (Jefferson City, MO), August 13, 1919; November 20, 1923; November 21, 1923; November 20, 1923.

Jefferson City (MO) Post-Tribune, September 17, 1924; July 15, 1930; March 17, 1932; September 27, 1938.

Jefferson City (MO) Tribune, May 28, 1926.

Jeffries, Jerry. *From Hog Alley to the Statehouse: A History of the Jefferson City Police Department*, *1836–1997*. Marceline, MO: Walsworth Publishing, 1998.

Missouri State Penitentiary Records. Missouri State Archives. Jefferson City, Missouri. https://s1.sos.mo.gov/records/archives/archivesdb/msp.

Sunday News and Tribune (Jefferson City, MO), December 27, 1936.

Chapter 6

Evening Missourian (Columbia, MO), March 30, 1918.

Find a Grave. "Susan Ing." March 2, 2009. www.findagrave.com.

Kansas City (MO) Sun, June 23, 1917; April 6, 1918; September 21, 1918.

Lincoln University Archives. Romeo West biography. Lincoln University. Jefferson City, Missouri.

Missouri Death Certificates. https://s1.sos.mo.gov/records/Archives/ ArchivesMvc/DeathCertificates.

Rising Son (Kansas City, MO), June 19, 1903.

Sedalia (MO) Weekly Conservator, June 17, 1905.

St. Joseph (MO) News-Press, October 14, 1912.

U.S. Census.

Chapter 7

Jefferson City (MO) News and Tribune, June 7, 1936.

Jeffries, Jerry. *From Hog Alley to the Statehouse: A History of the Jefferson City Police Department, 1836–1997*. Marceline, MO: Walsworth Publishing, 1998.

Kansas City (MO) Journal, December 27, 1896.

Kansas City (MO) Star, June 22, 1898.

Kansas City (MO) Times, April 29, 1897; June 22, 1898; June 23, 1898.

Potosi (MO) Journal, August 4, 1897.

South Western Reporter. "State v. Lanahan." St. Paul, MN: West Publishing Company, 1898.

Springfield (MO) News Leader, June 12, 1898.

St. Joseph (MO) Gazette, June 15, 1898.

St. Louis (MO) Globe-Democrat, June 12, 1898; June 22, 1898.

St. Louis (MO) Post-Dispatch, December 26, 1896; May 2, 1897; August 27, 1897; June 22, 1898.

Warrensburg (MO) Journal-Democrat, May 7, 1897.

Chapter 8

Daily Capitol News (Jefferson City, MO), January 6, 1923; January 10, 1923; January 14, 1923; February 28, 1923; April 11, 1923; April 12, 1923; May 20, 1923; September 7, 1924.

Jefferson City (MO) Post-Tribune, September 5, 1924; April 22, 1927; July 6, 1932.

Missouri Death Certificates. https://s1.sos.mo.gov/records/Archives/ ArchivesMvc/DeathCertificates.

Vintage Cole County Photos. "Wayne Johnson." https://vintagecolephotos. org/photographers.html.

Chapter 9

Daily Standard (Sikeston, MO), November 24, 1954.
Kirksville (MO) Daily Express, July 29, 1942.
St. Louis (MO) Globe Democrat, May 25, 1942; May 26, 1942; June 9, 1942.
St. Louis (MO) Post-Dispatch, December 12, 1958.

Chapter 10

State Journal (Jefferson City, MO), June 15, 1877; January 4, 1878; March 8, 1878; May 10, 1878; June 7, 1878; December 13, 1878.

Chapter 11

Ancestry. "New Orleans, Louisiana, U.S. Passenger Lists, 1813–1963." www.ancestry.com.
———. "U.S. and Canada Passenger and Immigration Lists Index, 1500s–1900s." www.ancestry.com.
Jefferson City (MO) News Tribune, Cole County History series.
Missouri's Union Provost Marshal Papers: 1861–1866. Missouri State Archives. Jefferson City, Missouri. https://s1.sos.mo.gov/records/archives/archivesdb/provost.
Peoples' Tribune (Jefferson City, MO), June 14, 1871.
Warrenton (MO) Banner, June 27, 1871.

Chapter 12

Crawford Mirror (Steelville, MO), December 18, 1879.
Fulton (MO) Gazette, January 17, 1879.
Jefferson City (MO) People's Tribune, October 23, 1878.
Missouri State Penitentiary Inmate Registers. Missouri State Archives. Jefferson City, Missouri. https://s1.sos.mo.gov/records/archives/archivesdb/msp.
State Journal (Jefferson City, MO), May 9, 1873; June 7, 1878; July 5, 1878; September 6, 1878; September 13, 1878; November 15, 1878.
St. Louis (MO) Globe-Democrat, January 6, 1879; January 14, 1879.

Chapter 13

Amick, Jeremy. "Allen Cemetery Provides Evidence of Guerilla Warfare during Civil War." Silver Star Families series. *Jefferson City (MO) News Tribune*, 2017.

Barnes, Joseph. *The Medical and Surgical History of the Civil War*. Wilmington, NC: Broadfoot Publishing Company, 1991.

Columbia (MO) Tribune, August 8, 2014.

Fairbanks, Jonathan, and Clyde Edwin Tuck. *Past and Present of Greene County, Missouri*. Indianapolis, IN: A.W. Bowen & Company, 1915.

Find a Grave. "Garrett Gabel." www.findagrave.com.

Fold3. "John Wilcox." Compiled Service Records. www.fold3.com.

Jeffries, Jerry. *From Hog Alley to the Statehouse: A History of the Jefferson City Police Department, 1836–1997*. Marceline, MO: Walsworth Publishing, 1998.

Legislative Manual and Political Directory. Olympia, WA: Wilson & Blankenship, 1899.

Million County Museum & Historical Society. "Surnames Beginning with 'W'." www.millercountymuseum.org.

Missouri Digital Heritage. Missouri Senate Journal, Regular Session. 1865. https://www.sos.mo.gov/mdh.

———. Soldiers' Records: War of 1812–World War I Database. https://www.sos.mo.gov/mdh.

National Park Service. "Battle Unit Details." https://www.nps.gov/index.htm.

Nichols, Bruce. *Guerrilla Warfare in Civil War Missouri*. Vol. 3, *January–August 1864*. Jefferson, NC: McFarland and Co., 2004.

———. Missouri in the Civil War message board. http://www.history-sites.com/cgi-bin/bbs62x/mocwmb/webbbs_config.pl.

Phelps County (MO) Focus, May 30, 2018.

Pryor, Joe. "Progress Notes." Miller County Museum & Historical Society. www.millercountymuseum.org.

U.S. Congressional Serial Set. Issue 3120, 1893, Special Order No. 141, HQ Dist of CeMo, Warrensburg 7/1/1864. https://www.govinfo.gov/help/serial-set.

Wood, Larry. "Civil War Execution of Johnn Wilcox." Missouri and Ozarks History. December 17, 2012. www.ozarks-history.blogspot.com.

Chapter 14

Ancestry.com. Undated clipping. www.ancestry.com.

———. U.S., Headstone Applications for Military Veterans, 1925–1970. www.ancestry.com.

———. World War I Draft Registration Cards, 1917–1918. www.ancestry.com.

Chalfant, Rhonda. "West End Saloon." National Register of Historic Places. 2014.

Cole County Democrat (Jefferson City, MO), November 15, 1906.

Daily Capital News (Jefferson City, MO), August 29, 1920; October 20, 1920; December 16, 1920; January 7, 1922; January 10, 1922; June 6, 1922; June 10, 1923; March 20, 1924; March 26, 1924; April 2, 1924; April 8, 1924; May 24, 1924; June 20, 1924; July 9, 1924; July 24, 1924; July 29, 1924; August 8, 1924; August 12, 1924; August 15, 1924; August 29, 1924; September 7, 1924; September 28, 1924; October 11, 1924; October 15, 1924; October 16, 1924; October 19, 1924; October 24, 1924; November 19, 1924; November 23, 1924; November 25, 1924; December 27, 1924; June 17, 1925; June 30, 1925; December 20, 1925; March 2, 1926; March 5, 1926; April 18, 1926; April 29, 1926; May 26, 1926; July 20, 1926; December 15, 1927; March 27, 1928; July 21, 1928; July 27, 1928; October 3, 1928; December 1, 1928; January 8, 1929; February 14, 1929; February 24, 1929; February 27, 1929; March 12, 1929; April 16, 1929; November 16, 1932; October 8, 1937.

Daily Democrat Tribune (Jefferson City, MO), December 6, 1911; May 24, 1924.

Daily Post (Jefferson City, MO), June 26, 1924; May 23, 1924; May 29, 1924, no. 270.

Jefferson City city directory. 1921; 1925. Missouri State Archives. https://www.sos.mo.gov/mdh/CityDirectories.

Jefferson City (MO) Post-Tribune, March 25, 1919; April 1, 1924; October 21, 1924; March 24, 1927; May 4, 1927; June 1, 1927; January 8, 1929; April 16, 1929; April 17, 1929; April 18, 1929; June 15, 1929; July 3, 1929; August 9, 1929; August 16, 1929; September 22, 1929; October 14, 1929; November 26, 1929; November 27, 1929; December 28, 1929; January 27, 1930; January 28, 1930; January 29, 1930; February 19, 1930; April 10, 1930; April 24, 1930; August 5, 1930; April 22, 1930; August 14, 1930; October 21, 1930; November 4, 1930; December 15, 1930; April 22, 1931; April 24, 1931; January 24, 1937; January 25, 1937; November 11, 1937; April 5, 1938; May 22, 1956.

Jefferson City (MO) Tribune, January 15, 1925; January 24, 1925; February 2, 1925; June 17, 1925; July 20, 1925; July 24, 1925; August 11, 1925; September 10, 1925; September 11, 1925; October 12, 1925; December 2, 1925; December 14, 1925; December 15, 1925; December 17, 1925; January 5, 1926; May 25, 1926; July 19, 1926; October 11, 1926; December 1, 1926; December 2, 1926; February 17, 1927; February 26, 1927; October 28, 1927; April 25, 1928; April 28, 1928; August 31, 1928; October 19, 1928; December 7, 1928; January 6, 1938.

Kansas City (MO) Star, November 26, 1929.

Kansas City (MO) Times, July 27, 1928.

Missouri Death Certificate. Missouri State Archives. Jefferson City, Missouri. https://s1.sos.mo.gov/records/Archives/ArchivesMvc/DeathCertificates.

St. Louis (MO) Post-Dispatch, November 26, 1929.

St. Joseph (MO) News-Press, January 28, 1930.

Sunday News and Tribune (Jefferson City, MO), July 7, 1935.

US Census.

Chapter 15

Argus (St. Louis, MO), July 25, 1924; August 1, 1924.

Daily Capitol News (Jefferson City, MO), Clipping 1923; August 24, 1923; October 2, 1923; October 3, 1923; October 24, 1923; July 4, 1924; July 13, 1924; July 22, 1924; July 24, 1924; July 29, 1924; August 28, 1924; August 31, 1924; September 3, 1924; September 30, 1924; November 16, 1924; November 23, 1924.

Democrat-Tribune (Jefferson City, MO), September 18, 1923; October 1, 1923; October 2, 1923; October 3, 1923.

Jefferson City (MO) Democrat-Tribune, September 18, 1923.

Jefferson City (MO) Tribune, February 18, 1926; April 10, 1926; April 15, 1926.

Rost, Sean. "A Call to Citizenship: Anti-Klan Activism in Missouri, 1921–1928." PhD diss., University of Missouri–Columbia, 2018.

Rustler (Russellville, MO), August 24, 1923.

St. Louis (MO) Post-Dispatch, February 14, 1924; February 15, 1924; October 7, 1924.

Chapter 16

Daily Capital News (Jefferson City, MO), July 17, 1924; September 26, 1924; October 1, 1924; October 10, 1924; November 18, 1924; November 20, 1924.

Jefferson City (MO) Tribune, June 14, 1926; November 9, 1926; November 29, 1926; December 2, 1926; January 25, 1927.

Missouri State Penitentiary Inmate Registers. Missouri State Archives. https://s1.sos.mo.gov/records/archives/archivesdb/msp.

Schreiber, Mark. *Somewhere in Time: 170 Years of Missouri Corrections*. Jefferson City, MO: Missouri Department of Corrections, 1991.

U.S. Census.

Chapter 17

Daily Capital News (Jefferson City, MO), March 27, 1930; March 28, 1930; March 29, 1930; March 30, 1930.

Jefferson City (MO) Post-Tribune, March 26, 1930; March 27, 1930; March 28, 1930; April 1, 1930.

Missouri National Guard Archives. Missouri State Archives. https://www.sos.mo.gov/archives/pubs/archweb/military.

Moberly (MO) Monitor-Index, March 26, 1930.

Revised Statutes of Missouri. Section 7374 Chapter 66. Missouri Revisor of Satutes. 1919. http://168.166.54.15/main/Home.aspx.

Sedalia (MO) Democrat, March 28, 1930.

Chapter 18

Brooks, Michelle. *Buried Jefferson City History*. N.p.: Kindle Direct Publishing, 2022.

Jefferson City (MO) Inquirer, June 17, 1841; July 1, 1841.

Jefferson City (MO) News Tribune, January 5, 1936.

Jeffersonian Republican (Jefferson City, MO), June 26, 1841.

Kuensting, B. "Barger Bullard info from Boone Co Mo." Unpublished manuscript, n.d.

Missouri House Journal, 1842. Jefferson City, Missouri. https://www.sos.mo.gov/archives/mdh_splash/default?coll=housesenatejrnls.

Schreiber, Mark. *Somewhere in Time: 170 Years of Missouri Corrections*. Jefferson City, MO: Missouri Department of Corrections, 1991.

Chapter 19

Ancestry. United States, Officer Down Memorials, 1791–2014. https://www.ancestry.com/search/collections/2373.

Jefferson City (MO) Post-Tribune, March 7, 1918.

Kansas City (MO) Star, September 13, 1921.

Missouri State Penitentiary Inmate Registers. Missouri State Archives. https://s1.sos.mo.gov/records/archives/archivesdb/msp.

Schreiber, Mark. *Somewhere in Time: 170 Years of Missouri Corrections*. Jefferson City, MO: Missouri Department of Corrections, 1991.

Sedalia (MO) Democrat, April 8, 1926; February 23, 1927.

St. Louis (MO) Star and Times, March 1, 1918.

St. Louis (MO) Globe-Democrat, November 15, 1923.

U.S. Census.

Chapter 21

Jefferson City (MO) News and Tribune, June 7, 1936.

Missouri State Penitentiary Inmate Registers. Missouri State Archives. https://s1.sos.mo.gov/records/archives/archivesdb/msp.

Potosi (MO) Journal, December 27, 1899.

Sedalia (MO) Democrat, August 5, 1900; January 21, 1902.

Southwest Mail (Nevada, MO), December 20, 1901.

St. Louis (MO) Post-Dispatch, January 5, 1902.

U.S. Census.

Chapter 22

Adair County Sheriff's Office. "History." Kirksville, MO. youradaircountysheriff.com/wordpress/289.html.

Ancestry. United States, Officer Down Memorials, 1791–2014. https://www.ancestry.com/search/collections/2373.

Benton-Scott County (MO) Kicker, May 8, 1909.

Boone County Government. "History of the Boone County Sheriff's Office." www.boonecountymo.org/sheriff/history.asp.

1883 History of Henry County, Missouri. Chapter 15. www.henrycomo.us/History/chap15.html.

Find a Grave. www.findagrave.com.

Henry County Democrat (Clinton, MO), November 30, 1905.

History of Henry and St. Clair Counties, Missouri. St. Joseph, MO: National Historical Company, 1883.

Howard County Sheriff's Office. Fayette, Missouri. www.hocomosheriff.com.

Iola (KS) Daily Record, November 25, 1905.

Jefferson City (MO) Post-Tribune, May 12, 1931.

Kansas City (MO) Star, November 27, 1905; June 21, 1907.

Kremer, Gary. *Heartland History: Essays on the Cultural Heritage of the Central Missouri Region.* St. Louis, MO: G. Bradley Publishing, 2000.

Linneus (MO) Bulletin, November 29, 1905.

Missouri State Penitentiary Inmate Registers. Missouri State Archives. https://s1.sos.mo.gov/records/archives/archivesdb/msp.

Missouri Supreme Court Reports. Vol. 200. Missouri State Archives. 1906.

Princeton (MO) Telegraph, October 5, 1904.

Santa Barbara (CA) Weekly Press, November 30, 1905.

Schreiber, Mark. *Somewhere in Time: 170 Years of Missouri Corrections.* Jefferson City, MO: Missouri Department of Corrections, 1991.

Sedalia (MO) Democrat, November 26, 1905.

Soldiers Database. Missouri State Archives. https://s1.sos.mo.gov/records/archives/archivesdb/soldiers.

Southwest Mail (Nevada, MO), July 5, 1907.

St. Louis (MO) Globe-Democrat, July 1, 1897; June 28, 1907.

St. Louis (MO) Republic, October 22, 1904.

Sunday News and Tribune (Jefferson City, MO), January 12, 1958.

Weekly Post (Nevada, MO), December 1, 1905.

INDEX

Crutcher, Esthus 99
Curry, Dr. W.A. 55

D

Damel, Reverend John 92
Dampf, Elliott 30
Dennis, Eugene 113
Dew, Lester 81
DeWyl, Dr. Nicholas 57
Diggs, Duke 35
Dupont, Leo 108

E

Edwards, Joseph 25
England 40, 123
Eveler, Henry 25
Eveler, Paul 83
Eveler, Tony 31
Ewing, Eber 74

F

Farris, William 73
Feil, John 22
Finn, Thomas 123
Fleeman, Captain C.L. 114
Ford, Joe 76
Fort Leavenworth, Kansas 71, 130
France 123
Francis, Edward 76
Frank, Nick 78
Fugate, James 123
Fuller, Lizzie 35
Fulton, Missouri 47

G

Gaines, Millie 44
Germany 122
Gibbs, J.A. 113
Gilvin, Porter 135
Glennon, Reverend John 94
Gmelich, Jacob 133
Goldman, Joseph 89
Gordon, John P. 93
governors
  Baker, Sam 35, 114
  Caulfield, Henry 116, 119
  Dockery, Alexander 128
  Donnell, Forrest 40
  Folk, Joseph 133
  Francis, David 60
  Hyde, Arthur 75, 91
  Lon Stephens 43
  Park, Guy 40
  Reynolds, Thomas 20, 124
  Stone, William 45
Graessle, Emil 100
Gray, William 38
Green Berry Bridge 72
Green, Leonard 133
Griesedieck Brewery Company 80
Griffin, Malcolm 30
Grundy County 131

H

Haas, Joe 24
Haas, Louis 133
Haas, Reverend Christian Ludwig 25
Haley, Sam 34, 75, 85, 90, 102
Hall, Matt 130
Hartman, John 54

Tritsch, Robert 38, 133
Tritsch, William 40

V

Vaughan, Harry 130
Vaughan, J.C. 70
Vernon County 137
Virginia 123, 134

W

Walthers, George 133
Warren County 96
Warrensburg 61
Weaver, R.E. 30
Weavers, William 75
Wegman, Jacob 130
West End Soft Drink Parlor 77, 79
Westhues, Judge Henry 49, 97, 102
Westphalia, Missouri 72
West, Professor Romeo 41
Wier, Harry 84
Wiggins, Floyd 76
Wilcox, John 61
Wilcox, Lucinda 63
Williams, Buck 135
Williams, C.G. 35
Williams, Emmett 34
Williams, J.G. 132
Wilson, L.M. 48
Wines, Captain T.J. 114
Winston, Dr. George 25
Winston, Dr. Willis 25, 55
Wisconsin 131
Wisener, John 113
Withaup, Augusta 103
Withaup, Sheriff Louis 35
Withaup Tire Repair Shop 96

Withaup, Walter 86, 98
Woehrman, Bill 82
Woodland, Charles 131
Woodruff, Harry 91
WOS 87

Y

Yaple, Lieutenant Lee 117
Young, Frank 127
Young, J.K. 131

ABOUT THE AUTHOR

Murder & Mayhem in Jefferson City is Michelle Brooks's fifth book. After nearly twenty-five years as a newspaper reporter, she has published *Hidden History of Jefferson City* and *Lost Jefferson City* with The History Press and self-published *Interesting Women of the Capital City* and coauthored *Buried Jefferson City History* with Nancy Thompson.

Brooks graduated from Lincoln University in 2018 with a bachelor of liberal studies degree with an emphasis in anthropology and history. She is a research analyst at the Missouri State Archives and is active in community history-related organizations.

She has lived in Jefferson City for more than twenty years and enjoys spending time with her family and gardening, when not writing and researching.

Visit us at
www.historypress.com
....